RIGHTEOUS LIVING

BY DR. TERESA ALLISSA CITRO

Raising Righteous Children

Righteous Living

Breathless Love

RIGHTEOUS LIVING

A BLESSED LIFE

TERESA ALLISSA CITRO, PH.D.

LINDA AGNES KNOWLES, PH.D.

JUSTIN NOAH CITRO, PH.D.

Edited by

TOBY PERELMUTER MARSHALL

RISE UP
PUBLICATIONS

Book and cover design by eBook Prep
www.ebookprep.com

July 2022
ISBN: 978-1-64457-316-7

Rise UP Publications
644 Shrewsbury Commons Ave
Ste 249
Shrewsbury PA 17361
United States of America
www.riseUPpublications.com
Phone: 866-846-5123

CONTENTS

This book is dedicated in loving memory to my father, Antonio Arcuri, who graduated into glory as I finished this book. My father lived a righteous life, and because of his strong faith, obedience, and convictions, he left a legacy in us, his children, and his grandchildren.

Dr. Teresa Allissa Citro

This book is dedicated in loving memory to my grandmothers Gina Bonafede and Agnes Lodato, the only women in my family who taught me what it meant to live a godly life and how to walk in righteousness before God.

Dr. Linda Agnes Knowles

This book is dedicated in loving memory of my Nonno, Antonio Arcuri, who was a great man of God. My grandfather taught me the ways on how to live righteously before God and how to obey the voice of the Lord.

Dr. Justin Noah Citro

ACKNOWLEDGMENTS

We wish to thank Rise UP Publications for their continued support and belief in our work. We thank our families for being patient and supportive as we wrote this book to bring glory and honor to our Lord Jesus Christ. This book would not have been possible without the editor at Rise UP Publications and Ellianna Destinee Citro for the countless hours they spent editing this book. Mostly, we thank you, the reader, for your desire to learn more about God's Word and live a righteous life. We love you.

INTRODUCTION

When I started writing this book, I thought I was writing about waiting on God. In the middle of writing, God completely changed the focus. Why am I sharing this with the reader? Because God showed me that the first thing we must do is live a life of righteousness. There is no point in expecting anything from God if we're not living righteously before Him.

Do you want to experience the blessings of God in your life? Do you want to see miracles worked in your family? Do you want God to hear and answer your prayers? If you have answered yes to all these questions, there is only one way to do this: by living a righteous life before God. This means obeying His Word. This means being holy as He is holy. There is no neutral ground when it comes to living for God. You are either living for Him or not. Psalm 34:17(KJV) says, *"The righteous cry, and the LORD heareth, and delivereth them out of all their troubles."* God is so gracious, so kind, and so merciful that He hears the cries of the righteous. He doesn't just hear them, but He delivers them out of all their troubles. The Hebrew word "natsal" is transliterated into the English word "delivereth," meaning "rescue or save." Did you catch that? God will rescue and save you from all those things that came to destroy you. He will make a way of escape in each and every situation that was meant to harm you. If that doesn't warrant living a righteous life, then I pray, as you study and discover the lives of the men and women in this book, you will be encouraged and spurred on, and you will desire to grow in righteousness so you, too, will be blessed and will have a life of fulfillment in Christ.

The Hebrew word "tsa`aq" is transliterated into the English word "yelled" meaning "to cry out in grief, cry out for help, shriek, cry out in distress or in need, to cry out for a wrong done to you." In keeping with being genuine and real, and speaking from the heart, I feel led to share a story with you. Normally, you write an introduction before you actually write the book. I didn't realize the introduction I originally wrote was about waiting on God.

After the book was finished, I came back to write the introduction. That's when it hit me that the Spirit of God isn't just speaking to me but also answering and showing me that living a life of righteousness is honorable. Let me explain. Six months ago, I was running on the beach in Daytona, Florida. As I was running, I was praying. Suddenly, I saw something that provoked a very painful memory. I began to cry. I had cried from my heart for eight years, asking God, "Why?" I just wanted the pain to go away. It is interesting to me how someone can say something out of the blue, or you can see something or even remember a scent that provokes a memory. When my eyes fell upon a place in front of me, the memories flooded my mind, and I started to sob. I was trying to control myself since I was in public. Thank God for sunglasses and a baseball cap. I stopped running; I couldn't catch my breath because I was crying. I saw a couple of people looking at me, wondering if I was okay. To me, my surroundings had blurred entirely around me. It was the overwhelming and overpowering picture in front of me. In that moment God spoke to me and said, "I can no longer take your weeping before me. Your tears have reached my nostrils, and I can no longer bear to see you suffer. I will not allow this to continue. Joy will be yours once again." I was comforted. I was immediately engulfed in the love of God, and I knew He was with me. Even though He allowed the suffering, He knew and reminded me that He was with me and there was hope for me. The crying had ended, and that's exactly what happened. I was a completely different person from that moment on. It was as if my heart didn't feel the pain anymore, and a new hope arose for my future. No wonder the above definition "to cry out in grief" humbled me.

You see, what God is saying is He *"...sendeth rain on the just and on the unjust,"* (Matthew 5:45 KJV). Living a righteous life doesn't exempt us from pain and suffering, from disasters and calamities, or from sicknesses and death. In other words, no believer can claim nothing bad is ever going to happen to them because to make such a statement is totally unbiblical; nor can we say that bad things happened because a person had no faith or that the person was not living righteously.

This book aims to show and teach us that God hears the call of the righteous. Job, the most righteous man who ever lived, said, *"Though he slay me yet will I trust him."* This is what it means. Job was a righteous man who had done no wrong, and tragedy after tragedy happened to him in a short time. Yet, God allowed it, but the victory became Job's victory. God heard Job's prayer in the stricken state he was in. God healed and restored Job, and God gave him double what he had lost. So it shall be with you and me as His Word states.

Whatever the cry of your heart is, you can be sure that God hears you. He sees your tears, and He can't bear to see His children in pain, distress, or heartache. He already has a plan of action to deliver you as we see in the lives of the people in this book. The Never-ending Oil of the Widow and Her Sons, the Courageous Abigail, the Mighty Warrior Caleb, and the Faithful Noah; these were all righteous people who had calamities and tragedies happen to them. They had people who opposed them, and they also dealt with those who tried to stop their blessing. However, the Lord delivered them out of all their troubles.

May you find strength and courage to rise up and live lives of righteousness. Second Timothy 3:16 (KJV) says, *"All scripture is given by inspiration of God, and is profitable for doctrine, for reproof, for correction, for instruction in righteousness."* Did you see that? The Scripture instructs on holy living, corrects, rebukes, and provides the teaching needed to live righteously because the Word of God is inspired by the Spirit of the living God.

"Surely he shall not be moved for ever: the righteous shall be in everlasting remembrance," (Psalm 112:6 KJV). I close with this Bible verse. No matter what happens in our lives, the righteous are never moved. Their roots run deep. They are trees planted by the water. They will always have green leaves regardless of the storms that come by. They are oaks of righteousness before a

righteous and holy God. There is a book of remembrance, and our Lord and Savior Jesus Christ has access to the book. The righteous are remembered. The righteous are saved. The righteous are hidden under His wings. The righteous shall prevail. The righteous are drawn to His side with everlasting love. Our prayer is that you will set your face like flint, determined to do His will and to live by His ways and His commands, knowing that you will not be brought to disgrace but will be called righteous. Our prayer is that you choose His will in all things.

CHAPTER 1
TRUSTING GOD
PART 1

The Poor Widow and Elisha

This story of the poor widow and Elisha fascinates me. We pray about seeing the glory of God, and in this story, we see the glory of God all over it. Do you know why? Because there was a man who was a true lover of God, a servant. He was a servant who obeyed, trusted, and had faith in God. He also taught it to his family. He provided a godly example for his family to see and follow. This godly man had died, but the legacy he left behind was a lasting one. The living God, who was in him, remained with his family. The Word of God clearly says in Psalm 37:25(KJV), *"I have been young, and now am old; yet have I not seen the righteous forsaken, nor his seed begging bread."* Did you catch that? The people around this widow and her sons were about to see the glory and splendor of God fully demonstrated in their family. My spirit within me is jumping for joy at what we are about to see in the life of this widow and her sons.

Let me give you a little background information relevant to the story. According to Exodus 21:2 (KJV), the law clearly says, *"If thou buy an Hebrew servant, six years he shall serve: and in the seventh he shall go out free for nothing."* Back in those days, the creditors were allowed to take the children and individuals into slavery until the debt was paid off or until the completion of the seventh year. This woman knew the fate of her children and herself. They had already come to threaten their future. She got up and went to see the prophet Elisha. Can't you feel and sense her firm and steadfast faith in her God? In 2 Kings 2:1 (KJV), it says, *"Thy servant my husband is dead; and thou knowest that thy servant did fear the Lord: and the creditor is come to take unto him my two sons to be bondmen."* Please clearly understand the first thing that she said. She acknowledged her deceased husband's faith and trust in the unfailing God. That tells me she understood her husband's seed would not be begging for bread or ending up in slavery. What happens next is the beginning of her seeing and experiencing for herself and then showing her sons the power, the might, and the deliverance given to those who serve Him in righteousness and obedience.

What Elisha did next went down as one of the greatest miracles in history. Elisha could have just given her what she needed, saving her sons and ending it there. However, that is not what God wanted. Because Elisha was a real prophet of God and led of the Spirit, we can see how he responded toward her in 2 Kings 4:2 (KJV), *"And Elisha said unto her, What shall I do for thee? tell me, what hast thou in the house?..."*

Elisha, led by the Spirit of God, was setting her up to see the glory of God manifested in one of the biggest miracles ever recorded. God is always interested in revealing His power and might in our lives. Had Elisha just given her the money to pay off her creditors, she would not have had money to take care of herself and her sons for the rest of her days. Elisha, through the Spirit, took what she had and used it as a resource in her hands to pay the creditors and have all that she needed for the rest of her days. Often, we temporarily bail people out in our hurry of wanting to do things our way. In doing so, it only takes care of the immediate problem, but in the long run, it hurts the person. You and I are not saviors in anyone's life. The real miracle is when God steps in and does the impossible. This is what took place in this story.

Immediately, the widow went home with no hesitation, no questioning, and no complaining. She went and did exactly what the prophet told her to do as we see in 2 Kings 4:3-4 (KJV), *"Then he said, Go, borrow thee vessels abroad of all thy neighbours, even empty vessels; borrow not a few."* You see, there was something she needed to do and that was to accept, believe, trust, and go. This is where many people miss it. When people are not given the resources upon request, many times, the initial reaction of some people, at this point, would be to throw a tantrum and blame the prophet for not helping. Because Elisha was in the spirit, he knew this would not be a one-time need. This widow and her sons would need food and money to survive for the rest of their lives. This meant that a miracle for them had to occur so they would be safe and provided for daily.

What happens next is very important. Elisha was very specific about what the widow and her sons needed to do. Let's look at each one and the significance of the tasks. First, they needed to borrow. I want us to pause at this word "borrow." The English word "borrow" means to take something from someone to return it back to the person who loaned it to you. In the original Hebrew, the word "sha'al" transliterates into English as the word "borrow." However, the word "sha'al" means something quite different in the Hebrew language compared to what the English word means. In the Hebrew language, it means "to inquire, to request, to demand." This means that the first thing they needed to do was ask. They needed to appeal, to make a call, and perhaps even beg for the pots. They were literally petitioning, pleading, and praying that those people would give them what they asked for. They urged their neighbors to give them the pots they needed and were persistent until they were acquired. Do you see that they used all methods given to them, describing this word "borrow," (sha'al)? This gives a completely different impression about borrowing in this story. Isn't that what we do when we come before the throne of God? We implement all those things to bring us our blessing. This means that, like the widow and her sons, we too must go to God. I venture to say that there wasn't a pot left in all of that town. They took possession of everything. This is a lesson for us when we pray; we go, petition, and take possession of the blessings. We should pause and take note of the word "borrow." Understanding this word should change everything for you and me. This word holds power.

Secondly, they needed to close the door. In 2 Kings 4:4 (KJV) it says, "*And when thou art come in, thou shalt shut the door upon thee and upon thy sons, and shalt pour out into all those vessels, and thou shalt set aside that which is full.*" The second mistake people make is when a word is spoken to them, and they go and blab to everyone else what God has told them in secret. I have been guilty of this. In my excitement over an amazing word I received, I shared it with other believers only to have them ridicule, make fun of, and tear down the promises God had spoken over my life. I believe we've all been there. In this story, we see a strong command by Elisha to do this in secret. I can think of several reasons why this was mandatory. They would not have been given the pots. There would have been a lot of jealous people out there who would have wanted to cash in on the blessing. The creditors were knocking on the door. The oil would not have been ready, or they would have been in the middle of the pouring. The flow would have stopped, and the creditors could have forcibly removed them into slavery before God was finished with His provision of the miracle. The miracle was specifically for the widow and her sons, not anyone else. You see, God was honoring the righteous. The righteous was their father who had passed away. However, the blessing was for his seed, his sons, and widow because they were also righteous before God.

Beloved brothers and sisters, be the man or woman of God demonstrating to your children how to be holy and righteous before the living, holy, and righteous God by living your lives in holiness before Him. Then you and your children shall lack no good thing. To the faithful, God will show Himself faithful.

Thirdly, it is important to note that her obedience played a major role in receiving the blessing for her and her sons. Let's note 2 Kings 4:5 (KJV), "*So she went from him, and shut the door upon her and upon her sons, who brought the vessels to her; and she poured out.*" Imagine for a moment if she didn't obey Elisha.

I would like to share a personal story about obedience. I was driving down a road in St. Cloud, Florida, heading for Melbourne Beach. My children and I were dressed in our beach attire, and I was praying in my mind. I was in the far-right lane and I saw a bank on the left, and God told me, "Get off the highway, and go to that bank." I was arguing with God, "I have no business in the bank. I'm dressed for the beach." And I still continued driving to the beach. Suddenly, I became ill, like I was going to faint. I went from the fourth lane to the far-left lane because that was the exit lane to the bank. I could not even believe there were no cars, allowing me to make a dramatic move across four lanes. My children were in shock. "Mom, what are you doing?" I said, "God wants me to go inside that bank." My children said, "Mom, we're not dressed for the bank. What do you have to do at the bank?" I had to be honest and tell them, "I have no clue, but God told me to go to the bank." We pulled into the parking lot, got out of the car, and went into the bank. My eyes fell on this man. God said, "You see that man? I want you to go over and talk to that man." I began to protest to God, and God said, "I told you to talk to that man." I told my children, "God told me to speak to that man, but I don't know what to say to him." My children were looking at each other, and like most children, they were thinking with their look that said, "Mom, please don't embarrass us." I continued to pray in my mind a lot harder and stronger. Then the receptionist walked over to me and asked, "How may we help you?" In my mind, I asked the Lord, "God, what do I say?" He said, "Tell her you want to change your signature card." That bought me some time. She said, "Please sit down and wait for the next available representative." Ten people were representatives that day. God told me to get in line and make a deposit. So, I got in line trying to make a deposit, keeping my eye on the man I was going to speak to and trying to figure out how I would tell that woman that I only wanted to talk to the man over there. The people in front of me who were waiting for their turn heard the woman suddenly say to me, "You're next, and the representative you will be talking to is over..." and she pointed to the man God wanted me to talk to. I had never jumped out of a line so fast. My children, who were observing in complete shock, went to sit down. The man, whose name was Lee, shook my hand, and as I sat down, he asked, "How may I help you?" I said, "Well, I'm here to change my signature card." He said, "What is your name?" And I replied, "The name of the organization is Thread of Hope, Inc." He leaned back in his chair and said, "Hmmm, tell me about Thread of Hope." So, I told him about Thread of Hope, and his next statement stunned me. He said, and I quote, "So, you are the person that God has sent me to this bank to help. I have been waiting six months for you." Now it's a good thing, people, that I was sitting in the chair, or I think I would have passed out. If you can, imagine my children's mouths hanging open and their eyes bulging out as I turned around and said, "This is why we obey the voice of the Lord." I explained to Lee what I just explained here. Lee introduced me to the woman, the first jeweler. The latter would help me create my bracelet design which launched my fine jewelry collection. That relationship led me to design my first piece of jewelry in what is now called "Citro Collections Fine Jewelry." That needed to happen before I received the second and third steps that led me to fulfill the call of God to design and produce Forever Yours by Citro Collections, my own line of engagement rings and wedding bands. Do you see how God works? God directed Lee to go work at this specific bank because God was sending someone that Lee needed to help. He was on guard, looking and waiting for the person to come. I was that person. It required obedience on his and my part. Now again, I say to you that obedience is better than sacrifice. This is what the widow did in this story with her sons and a modern-day example of what I did.

Lastly, in this story, the widow starts to pour from the jar that she possessed already. You see, she already possessed her provision. She was exercising her faith and trusting God at this point. Can you see it? ...jars everywhere. She started to pour into the first jar, but that was not a shock because she knew the oil was already in the jar. She took the second jar, and she filled that one. Can you imagine when she got to the point when she knew that there was not supposed to be that amount in her original jar? Can you see the eyes of her children bulging out and their mouths hanging open? Can you see her trembling in awe of the miracle before her very eyes? Those pots kept coming and the oil held off until each pot that her sons collected was filled, the pots that they collected with their persistence, begging, and pleading until there were no pots left in the town. That is the ultimate example of persistence and obedience. What a story! What a miracle!

Observe this. In 2 Kings 4:6 (KJV), it says, *"And it came to pass, when the vessels were full, that she said unto her son, Bring me yet a vessel. And he said unto her, There is not a vessel more. And the oil stayed. Then she came and told the man of God. And he said, Go, sell the oil, and pay thy debt, and live thou and thy children of the rest."* Please take note: the Hebrew word for "stayed," in 2 Kings 4:6 (KJV), is "`amad" which means, "to stand, remain, endure." I want you to know that when I started to write this chapter, the first thing the Holy Spirit told me was "Look up the word 'stayed' in Hebrew because that word does not mean what you think it means or what the messages you have heard say." So, in essence, the word "stayed" in English is not the same as the Hebrew word "`amad" which means it outlasted. It went on and on. It remained. It held. It never ran out. Are you seeing what I'm seeing? The oil was persistent in multiplying, never stopping. It was used to sustain the widow and her sons so they could survive. In other words, in plain old English, it outlasted and outlived the widow and her sons. The miracles of God prevail, remain, and linger on and on just like the oil. The anointing of God is what preserves, safeguards, and secures us. Isn't that what God was doing for the widow and her sons? He preserved the widow's oil and multiplied it and kept it going for the rest of her life. Clearly, that was God's provision for her. He safeguarded them from their creditors, which means He protected them so no one could bring them harm by capturing them into slavery. God secured the widow and her sons by ensuring the oil kept going, giving them stability, peace of mind, safety, and a living wage because she could sell the oil. It was King David who declared, in Psalm 119:165 (KJV), *"Great peace have they which love thy law: and nothing shall offend them."* Do you know what this means? When you love God's law and obey Him, nothing will be a stumbling block to you.

In conclusion, there was a man who was righteous before God, and even though we don't know his name, we know this one vital fact of his life: he was a righteous man who feared God. God saved this man's widow and his seed. Isn't this what we all desire?

Listen carefully, please. The widow knew God would come through for her. She continued living a righteous life before God and trusting in the God she served. As a result, God honored her faith. He proved to her that His grace was sufficient for her and would carry her through all the days of her life. This didn't just include her. This included her sons as well. Because of her, they had another godly example of righteousness and faith lived out before them as they saw the miracle of oil being multiplied. They had more than enough.

This is something we should aspire to. We should live such godly and righteous lives that God's favor will remain upon us and sustain us for the rest of our lives. There is only one way to gain God's favor, the widow understood this clearly. Righteousness in the eyes of God, along with obeying His commands and laws, covers you with grace and favor lavished upon you by God.

Study Guide

As we see in the story of the widow, righteousness plays an important role in the life of a believer. We are commanded to be holy as God is holy and we are to be perfect as God is perfect. In the King James Bible, the words "righteous" and "righteousness" are mentioned approximately 555 times. Clearly, righteousness is an essential theme in the pages of the Bible. God still commands those who are His children to live holy and righteous lives. When we are doing what God requires, we are doing what is right, and in doing that, we are pleasing God. In 1 John 2:29 (KJV), it says, *"If ye know that he is righteous, ye know that every one that doeth righteousness is born of him."* The righteous are blessed by God, but those who live to gratify the lusts of their flesh pay in disastrous consequences. 1 Samuel 15:22 (KJV) says, *"...Behold, to obey is better than sacrifice..."* This widow and her family lived by the laws of God and walked before God with pure hearts, and God honored them with protection and provision. He lavished His grace and mercy upon them. *"And it shall be our righteousness, if we observe to do all these commandments before the Lord our God, as he hath commanded us,"* (Deuteronomy 6:5 KJV).

1. The widow exercised her faith in God by living a life of righteous before Him. What did she do that demonstrated that she lived a righteous life?

2. As a prophet of God, Elisha played a role in this woman receiving her miracle. He had instructed her with godly counsel and told her step by step what needed to be done. What act was vital for the widow to perform and why?

3. In 2 Kings 4:4 (KJV), it says, *"And when thou art come in, thou shalt shut the door upon thee and upon thy sons, and shalt pour out into all those vessels, and thou shalt set aside that which is full."* What are some possible reasons for Elisha telling the widow to close the door behind her and her sons?

4. Keeping in mind the widow's story, read Matthew 5:6 (KJV): *"Blessed are they which do hunger and thirst after righteousness: for they shall be filled."* Explain this verse.

5. As we have seen in the widow's life, God does far beyond

what we could ever ask or imagine. Too often, we limit the blessings of God due to lack of faith. In Ephesians 3:20 (KJV), it says, *"Now unto him that is able to do exceeding abundantly above all that we ask or think, according to the power that worketh in us."* Explain what this verse means to you.

CHAPTER 2
TRUSTING GOD
PART 2

Tamar, Judah's Daughter-in-Law

We learned from the widow's life of righteousness what can be accomplished when we obey God. Now we see another widow who took matters into her own hands for God's law to be fulfilled. Although God, in His mercy, compassion, and love, can turn any situation, circumstance, or sin into blessings, it does not excuse bad behavior, nor does it make sin unpunishable. Some consequences follow for every poor choice, decision, or sin one commits. None of us are exempt from the consequences of our actions.

Look at the story of another widow named Tamar in Genesis 38:1-30 (KJV). Because of the length of this passage, we will be highlighting particular verses. In Genesis 38:1-2 (KJV), it says, *"And it came to pass at that time, that Judah went down from his brethren, and turned in to a certain Adullamite, whose name was Hirah. And Judah saw there a daughter of a certain Canaanite, whose name was Shuah; and he took her, and went in unto her."* That's the first mistake. He went to a place where he should not have been, and while there he took a wife, not just any woman, but a Canaanite, going against his father and grandfather's wishes. To be perfectly clear, this also went against what Abraham had told his servant when looking for a wife for Isaac. There is a vital statement that Isaac made to Jacob, Judah's father, in Genesis 28:1 (KJV), *"So Isaac called for Jacob and blessed him. 'Do not take a wife from the Canaanite women,' he commanded."* By taking a Canaanite woman as his wife, he set up himself and his future children for the curses of the disobedience he had committed. Marrying a Canaanite was only the beginning of the destruction that would follow. Please do not be deceived. Disobedience always leads to destruction.

Let's continue with this story and see the results of his disobedience.

Judah's wife, Shuah gave birth to three sons named Er, Onan, and Shelah. Being a Canaanite woman, Shuah did not teach her sons about the God of Abraham, Isaac, and Jacob, the patriarchs of their family. Catch this: this was only the fourth generation. How long does it take for a godly generation to become ungodly? One person decides to go against the law of the living and true God. This is why we, as parents, must teach our children to obey the Lord and His law. We are told to *"Bind them upon thy fingers, write them upon the table of thine heart,"* (Proverbs 7:3 KJV). Let me explain the meaning of this verse to see the sin Judah committed by marrying a Canaanite. She was incapable of teaching her sons God's laws. You see, "tying God's laws to their hands" means that they wore a leather box containing parchment strips with four texts: Exodus 13:1-10,

Exodus 13:11-16, Deuteronomy 6:4-9, Deuteronomy 11:13-21. So, a box would be tied around the arm three times and then continue to be wound around the middle finger, and then whatever was left of the tie would be wound around the hand. This is what is meant when it says to tie the commandments of God around the fingers and hands. This is how much reverence they had for God's laws.

In Proverbs 6:21, it says, *"Bind them continually upon thine heart, and tie them about thy neck."* This is believed to mean the wearing of ornaments hanging around the neck. We need to pay careful attention to the commandments, the precepts, and the laws, and keep them in the front of our minds and written on our hearts so we will obey them and walk in His ways.

Godly parents take this seriously, especially mothers who taught their children to be righteous and holy before God. Judah did not take the teachings of his mother, Leah, into consideration. His actions led to what happens next with his sons.

In Genesis 38:6-7, it says, *"And Judah took a wife for Er his firstborn, whose name was Tamar. And Er, Judah's firstborn, was wicked in the sight of the Lord; and the Lord slew him."* Did you see what happens here? This is different from what happened to the widow and her sons. The widow's husband was a righteous man. Tamar's husband was a wicked man, and God just killed him. The custom in certain sects of Judaism, which is still followed today, is if a woman is widowed, the brother of the widow's dead husband takes care of her by marrying her. You would think that the second son, her new husband, would have been a better choice for Tamar. Unfortunately, that is not what happened. What took place next was disgusting and pure evil before the eyes of God. In Genesis 38:8-10, it says, *"And Judah said unto Onan, Go in unto thy brother's wife, and marry her, and raise up seed to thy brother. And Onan knew that the seed should not be his; and it came to pass, when he went in unto his brother's wife, that he spilled it on the ground, lest that he should give seed to his brother. And the thing which he did displeased the Lord: wherefore he slew him also."* One would think that the second son would have been fearful by his behavior towards right and wrong. So, here's the problem: disaster, destruction, and death follow the ungodly. God killed the second husband for his despicable act. It was really important for Tamar to have a child for two major reasons: (1) The child would be an heir. This would mean Er, Judah's oldest son, would inherit a major bulk of the inheritance upon Judah's death, and (2) It would assure her place in the family. Clearly, the Bible states that both young men were evil. So much so, that God took both of their lives. Their mother didn't teach them the ways of the Lord. They didn't wear the law of God on their hands or around their neck. They didn't adorn themselves with the ornaments of godly and righteous behavior, which would have led to blessings, honor, respect, and integrity. This is what it means when there is disobedience from the very start.

Unfortunately, the disaster continues and only gets worse. How much worse can it get? There is a third son whose name is Shelah. Judah, now wholly devastated by the death of his two eldest sons, decides to withhold the younger one with the excuse that he is not old enough to marry. One would think Judah would be inquiring of the Lord as to what in the world is happening. That should tell us the condition of his own heart. There is no way anyone can hear from God, be led of God, and do the will of God when they are living in sin. Judah promised Tamar the third son once he came of age, but he had no intention of doing so. He lied and betrayed Tamar, causing her to stumble and fall, resorting to the absolutely unthinkable. Since he had no intention of giving her Shelah, Judah himself was not a man of integrity or great character. He was not following the law of God, so how could his sons follow the law of God when he, the father, had not set the example? Because of his unrighteousness, his sons paid the price, which was punishment by the vengeance of God that killed them before their time. Judah, Er, and Onan were not righteous men.

Tamar was sent to live with her father until Shelah came of age. Shelah became of age, and Judah did not follow through in giving Shelah to Tamar. Judah's wife watched this whole thing happen before her eyes and was still not following the laws of God. Why would she? Judah had no business marrying a Canaanite woman. They were wholly unyoked. Before we go any further, let me be very clear. Who we marry determines the blessings of God or the curses that are set for those who would dare defy the living God. We might live after the law and in the age of grace, but God will never look the other way regarding sins or ungodly behavior. The commandments, the precepts, and the law of God still stand. They have not changed even in this age of grace. The Word of God clearly tells us that God will spit us out of His mouth if we are lukewarm. Eventually, Shuah, Judah's wife, died. Tamar cooked up a plan of action that turned out to be more righteous than the man who was to be one of the twelve tribes of Israel. Sometimes, those who are not believers act godlier than those who claim to have a relationship with God.

"And it was told Tamar, saying, Behold thy father in law goeth up to Timnath to shear his sheep. And she put her widow's garments off from her, and covered her with a veil, and wrapped herself, and sat in an open place, which is by the way to Timnath; for she saw that Shelah was grown, and she was not given unto him to wife. When Judah saw her, he thought her to be an harlot; because she had covered her face. And he turned unto her by the way, and said, Go to, I pray thee, let me come in unto thee; (for he knew not that she was his daughter in law.) And she said, What wilt thou give me, that thou mayest come in unto me?" (Genesis 38:13-16 KJV). It is so sad that Judah did not learn his lesson. Here he is again going somewhere and making another unwise decision. Tamar sizes up the situation, seizes the opportunity, and entraps her father-in-law to ensure the continuation of the rightful heir to Judah's estate and assure her place in the family. Let's take note of something right here.

When Judah found his Canaanite wife, Shuah, it was at Hirah the Adullamite's place. Now the wife died, and he went back to hang out at Hirah the Adullamite's place. Righteous men make righteous and wise decisions. Unrighteous men make unrighteous and unwise decisions. He obviously didn't learn anything from the first time around. This is how far he was from God. Now I want to point out something else. Everyone around Tamar knew that her father-in-law was not doing right by her and was not doing right in the eyes of God. The question is, what would cause Tamar to dress as a prostitute to entrap her father-in-law? Godly men do not go around hiring the services of a prostitute. Obviously, she knew the character of her father-in-law, and she was going to use it for her benefit.

For Tamar to be free to marry, she needed to have a child by Judah or remain with Judah. You see, ungodly behaviors always lead to ungodly actions. Had Judah done right in the beginning of his life, we wouldn't find this story, which is repulsive. Sin causes people to be foolish, as in this case with Judah. He had no idea that it was Tamar who he was with. When she asked him for forms of identification, he just handed them over without any questions. So, he gave her the signet (his seal) with its cord and the staff, all considered forms of identification. This is equivalent of us just handing over our passport or driver's license. She literally had his identification seal. Again, he had no idea who she was, but he handed over the items she would later use to identify him.

What amazes me is his quick judgment to burn her at the stake when he finds out that she is with child. In this distasteful and ungodly story, finally, we find Judah doing the right thing. He admits his sin, acknowledges that he should have given her Shelah, and even says what Tamar did was more righteous than him. Eventually, as recorded in 1 Chronicles 4:21, we find that Shelah names his first son "Er." This shows us that he had entered the levirate marriage with his sister-in-law, Tamar, producing the heir for his eldest brother named "Er." While Tamar may have produced an heir for her late husband, we cannot say that God approved of her methods. There is no Scripture found where Tamar, like the widow, went to any prophet or sought out godly counsel. According to the Word of God, when we acknowledge our wrongdoing and turn from our evil ways, doing what is right and pleasing before the eyes of

God, there is forgiveness. In this Judah and Tamar debacle, we find a surprising blessing. We can find them in the lineage of King David, and then we find them eventually in the lineage of Jesus Christ, the King of kings.

We find very vital truths in these two stories of the two widows and the men involved. Both the righteous and the unrighteous have many problems, but the Lord delivers the righteous from all their problems. He blesses, increases, and keeps them in their day of trouble. The first widow, who we have no name for, had a righteous husband, and God provided for her and her children for the rest of her life. Can you imagine the oil never running out? She was completely taken care of with no shame, no deception, and no drama. Tamar, on the other hand, was a part of unrighteous men who caused her embarrassment, shame, and almost cost her her life. The difference between the two women is night and day. We are to lead lives of right-eousness. In doing so, it's like a mirror. The Lord Himself shall show His righteousness.

Study Guide

As we see in the story of Tamar, "...*sin is a reproach to any people,*" (Proverbs 14:34 KJV). Sin doesn't affect just the individual committing the sin, but the sinning person affects everyone around them. You will see this in the other chapters as well. Sin separates a person from God. Unless sin is confessed and repented of before God, the person remains unrighteous, stained with the guilt of sin. Tamar had been married to Er, Judah's oldest son, and Er was an evil man. He was so evil that God took his life. Then Onan became Tamar's husband, didn't obey God, and was as evil as his brother, Er. God took Onan's life. Now Judah had one other son left, Shelah, whom he promised to Tamar. Judah broke his word and broke God's law, and we see a spiral of wicked events spun out of control because Judah decided to disobey God and His law. Judah could have done the right thing, but he chose not to, and we see the consequences of that sin. Tamar was greatly affected by Judah's sin of disobedience. As a result, she resorted to drastic and dramatic measures to have children after seeing that Shelah was of age to be married and that Judah had withheld Shelah from her. Rather than trusting God for what was rightfully hers, she literally took matters into her own hands and conceived twins with Judah. She almost ended up being killed for it. Note the difference between her and the widow whom Elisha had helped: the widow had trusted in God even though the circumstances put her in a critical situation, versus Tamar, who helped God out and resorted to her own ways to bring about producing an heir.

1. What was the first sin Judah committed, and why was it a sin?

2. Tamar was married to Er and Onan, who were evil men. Why was it so important and critical for Tamar, upon the death of her first husband, to produce an heir for her late husband Er?

3. *"Bind them upon thy fingers, write them upon the table of thine heart,"* (Proverbs 7:3 KJV). What is the significance of this? As children of God, how do we demonstrate that the laws of God are written in our hearts?

4. Matthew 7:1-3 (KJV) says, *"Judge not, that ye be not judged or with what judgment ye judge, ye shall be judged: and with what measure ye mete, it shall be measured to you again. And why beholdest thou the mote that is in thy brother's eye, but considerest not the beam that is in thine own eye?"* How can this passage of Scripture be applied to Judah's situation when he quickly judged Tamar for being pregnant and then had to back down when he was handed the items that identified him as the father of her twins?

5. What blessing resulted from the disastrous Judah and Tamar debacle?

CHAPTER 3
LIVE YOUR LIFE
PART 1

Abigail

The story of Abigail and Nabal disturbs me a great deal.

We find a godly woman with godly actions led by God, respecting, honoring, and loving a complete fool. She was fearless and stood her ground, did the right thing no matter what the cost, and took matters into her own hands to stop the destruction that was about to occur. It sounds to me that she measures up to the woman spoken about in Proverbs 31. However, Nabal, her husband, was wicked and unrighteous before God. He was rude, unappreciative, unkind, and a drunkard. No wonder his name means "fool," a real foolish man. What a contrast between him and his wife.

Let's take a deeper look into this story in I Samuel 25:1-44 (KJV), starting with the first four verses, "...*And David arose, and went down to the wilderness of Paran. And there was a man in Maon, whose possessions were in Carmel; and the man was very great, and he had three thousand sheep, and a thousand goats: and he was shearing his sheep in Carmel. Now the name of the man was Nabal; and the name of his wife Abigail: and she was a woman of good understanding, and of a beautiful countenance: but the man was churlish and evil in his doings; and he was of the house of Caleb."*

Nabal was not an ordinary man. He was a man of possession, power, and wealth. He was in a position to make a difference in the life of David, who was a man of God and a future king whom God had appointed and anointed. In addition, and most importantly, Nabal was in the lineage of Caleb.

In the previous chapter, I said, "How long does it take for a godly generation to become an ungodly generation?" We see it repeated here in this story. Nabal was of the household of Caleb. Caleb wasn't just an ordinary person. Remember Caleb? He and Joshua were two of the twelve spies sent to investigate the land, the only two whom God honored because of their faith, who saw the Promised Land. Caleb said to Joshua to give him the mountain, signifying that he still trusted God to get to the top of the mountain and conquer it completely. That mountain was Mount Hebron. Nabal was now the proud owner of Caleb's godly and righteous behavior.

Unfortunately, Nabal did not inherit or possess the most essential qualities like his ancestor Caleb. It fascinates me to see the length God goes through to bless people who don't deserve it. I see this too often in people's lives. Many throw away the godly influences of their parents, grandparents, and other family members throughout their lineage.

It is stories like this and the previous one of Judah and Tamar that absolutely scare me in a good way. If we are not careful, we too, can lose our inheritance here on Earth and, most importantly, our inheritance in Heaven, like we see here with Nabal. No wonder the Word of God says to work out your salvation with fear and trembling.

Where was Nabal's tie around his hand and arm? Why were the precepts not hung around his neck? Didn't he know the story of his lineage and who Caleb was? Didn't he see the blessing of the Lord? Wasn't he the one who inherited Mount Hebron? Wasn't it entrusted into his hands? Caleb was a visionary. He was a faithful man. He was righteous. He was honorable. He fought the good fight, conquered his enemies, won the battle, and possessed the land. That is who was in Nabal's lineage, and the reason it's upfront in his story is to remind us of what family he came from. Personally, I am very much into names and their importance. I am obsessed with it.

Neither of my children were named after family members, which is the Italian tradition, but rather after meanings of whom God told me they were to be. Let me give you an example: Nabal means "fool." Imagine his parents, grandparents, aunts, and uncles, cousins, friends, and town people calling out his name: "Hi, Fool!" "Fool, come here." Let's compare that to my daughter's name, Ellianna, and my calling her by her name. "God has answered me." "The Lord has responded." Do you see the importance of naming children names that remind them and us of who they are? Nabal's parents named him a fool, and that is who he became, and it cost him his life.

Let's look at 1 Samuel 25:5-9 (KJV), *"And David sent out ten young men, and David said unto the young men, Get you up to Carmel, and go to Nabal, and greet him in my name: And thus shall ye say to him that liveth in prosperity, Peace be both to thee, and peace be to thine house, and peace be unto all that thou hast. And now I have heard that thou hast shearers: now thy shepherds which were with us, we hurt them not, neither was there ought missing unto them, all the while they were in Carmel. Ask thy young men, and they will shew thee. Wherefore let the young men find favour in thine eyes: for we come in a good day: give, I pray thee, whatsoever cometh to thine hand unto thy servants, and to thy son David. And when David's young men came, they spake to Nabal according to all those words in the name of David, and ceased."*

We see the godly actions and reactions of a godly and righteous man named David in this passage. Notice how he addresses Nabal. First, he acknowledges the blessings of God on his life and property. Undoubtedly, David knew who Caleb was. He would have heard the stories of how the Israelites possessed the Promised Land that Nabal was enjoying. With respect, honor, and integrity, David was reminding Nabal who he was. David was running from King Saul. Everyone would have known that information. David knew that there was a call on his life, and eventually, he, too, like Caleb, would have to take his promises and possess the land that God was giving him. He was coming with peace to the household and land of Nabal. In other words, David was not coming as a warrior just to take what belonged to someone else, particularly to Nabal in this case.

Secondly, David came using the word "peace" throughout his introductory information for Nabal and said, *"Peace be both to thee, and peace be to thine house, and peace be unto all that thou hast."* Look at how David began each of those with the word "peace." David had no ill will, and he was not coming to start any kind of trouble. Let me explain. David was not asking

Nabal for something unheard of at that time. It was a perfectly normal customary practice that a request like that of David would be accepted and given. During the sheep shearing times, they would hold great feasts, which meant they were celebrating, and there was lots of food to go around, more than what they could actually eat. Therefore, there was more to be shared. David and his men knew it, Nabal and his men knew it, and everyone around them knew it. David, being godly, even prepared his men to deliver the message with respect, honor, and class. David didn't have to do that. That is the point. He and his men could have just shown up. In my opinion, God gave David the knowledge and wisdom to send his men in respect for Nabal and his herdsmen. Before we continue in the story, let me stop here and give you a gold nugget. It is God and only God that knows the heart and its intent. God already knew how Nabal would react, yet God was being good, compassionate, kind, loving, and slow to anger. God was literally allowing Nabal to do what was right. Isn't it like God to give us chance after chance until we have exhausted His mercy and grace? We can see in Nabal's response the wickedness and unrighteousness that filled his heart, mind, and soul. It spills out in 1 Samuel 25:10 (KJV), *"And Nabal answered David's servants, and said, Who is David? and who is the son of Jesse? there be many servants now a days that break away every man from his master."* There was absolutely no reason for Nabal to respond so insolently to David.

David was well-known. He was talked about, and even the Philistines knew that David had killed thousands. David's successes spread like wildfire. Instead of treating David with the same respect that David had treated him with, Nabal, without a thought, treated David like he was some slave or vagabond that got away from his master. He treated David like a dog. David did nothing to deserve that treatment from Nabal because he had blessed Nabal, his home, and all he had by saying, "peace." Let's not forget that David also protected Nabal's shepherds, herdsmen, and all that Nabal possessed from any surrounding groups of people who could have hurt them. David and his men acted as a wall of protection around them. No one could touch them. Instead of meeting David with returned kindness, Nabal not only turned down his request but also repaid David's kindness with evil. To add insult to injury, one more major note is that David and Nabal were both from the same tribe. Can you believe the audacity, arrogance, and ungrateful attitude of Nabal? No wonder he was a fool. Nabal lived up to his name very well: "Fool."

Here's how David reacted to what Nabal said. His response is found in 1 Samuel 25:13 (KJV), *"And David said unto his men, Gird ye on every man his sword. And they girded on every man his sword; and David also girded on his sword: and there went up after David about four hundred men; and two hundred abode by the stuff."* David was never a man to allow wrong to take place. He was a fearless type of man. In this case, it had nothing to do with taking something by force. It had to do with the disrespectful answer that Nabal had given David. You see, it's all about respect and honor. Nabal was disrespecting and dishonoring one of his relatives, and what was worse was that David protected Nabal. David knew how to protect and take care of his own. Sometimes I wonder if David didn't already know about the integrity and character of Nabal. In my opinion, it is difficult to observe and not see the characters of those around us. It's almost as if David tried to push "peace" with Nabal so that Nabal would get the hint since David had repeated it three times.

Parents know this well. It is a fact that when you repeat the same thing to your child three times, you are sending a message. Arrogant and wicked Nabal ignored the peace. Here lies the true foolishness of this man. Surely, Nabal knew of David's victories over his enemies. He would have had to have known that his actions would evoke anger and retaliation in David and his men. He knew the message he sent back to David was that of war, and David rose to the occasion. David was angry, insulted, and desperate; he and his men were hungry. Nabal's foolishness was now going to cause a bloodbath.

Foolish people do not consider their own lives. When they don't consider their own lives, they will not consider the lives of their family, friends, or anyone else around them. In Proverbs 15:1-2 (KJV), it says, *"A soft answer turneth away wrath: but grievous words stir up anger. The tongue of the wise useth knowledge aright: but the mouth of fools poureth out foolishness."*

Thank God for a woman of wisdom and godly actions like Abigail. When Abigail was told by their herdsman about what happened, her response was immediate and quick, according to the account in 1 Samuel 25:18-19 (KJV), *"Then Abigail made haste, and took two hundred loaves, and two bottles of wine, and five sheep ready dressed, and five measures of parched corn, and an hundred clusters of raisins, and two hundred cakes of figs, and laid them on asses. And she said unto her servants, Go on before me; behold, I come after you. But she told not her husband Nabal."* Abigail assessed the situation very quickly. She knew the consequences that

Nabal had just brought upon their home and possessions and those working for her and Nabal. Let me tell you, that was not a small amount of food. She provided everything they would need and then gave extra. She didn't wait around, ask permission, discuss it, or go into prayer. She did the right thing at the right time and did so promptly. In the eyes of God, Abigail had done the right and admirable thing. Abigail was every man's dream.

I want to point out three significant things in the actions of Abigail. The first point is that she protected her husband even though he didn't deserve it. By Abigail's actions, she kept her husband from being killed. A woman of character and virtue is, as the Bible says, a crown on her husband's head. It amazes me that God had given Nabal, who was a fool, a woman of wisdom, character, integrity, class, and beauty. It shows that some individuals will never appreciate God's greatest blessings. The second point is that she was quick-thinking, and she put together a meal fit for a king. She was not an ordinary woman. She quickly put together a meal at a moment's notice, and it wasn't an ordinary one. It was from soup to nuts. In other words, she spared nothing, and to top it off, it was for six hundred men. That is a lot of men to feed at the last minute. Finally, notice how she first sent the men and donkeys with the food. That was brilliant, but I don't expect anything less from this woman Abigail. Abigail knew that first you meet the need. There is no sense in reasoning until you show that you mean business. Abigail knew the seriousness of the situation, she met the need first, then she arrived.

Picture this with me: David was enraged, and this anger transferred to his men. Now you have six hundred angry men, and four hundred men ready and suited up to attack. On the horizon, they look and behold, before them is an entourage of men and donkeys coming toward them. We're not talking about two or three donkeys. There would have been many loaded with the supplies and food necessary to take care of six hundred men. First came the bread, then came the meat, the wine, and the raisins and figs. Can you imagine this sight and the shock that came over David and his men?

And then came this beautiful woman riding on a donkey. She comes down off the donkey and falls prostrate before David and his men coming towards her. What a sight to behold! She was fearless, bold, humble, and respectful. Go, Abigail, go! We can learn a lot from her actions. The next thing that happens in this scene, Abigail petitions him and throws herself at his mercy. She made no excuses. She was not hysterical. She was not scared, and she didn't lie about anything. She recognized who David was, and she recognized who her husband was. She spoke truth. I am so impressed with this woman of honor and integrity that I am going to include her entire speech to David found in 1 Samuel 25:24-31 (KJV), "...*Upon me, my lord, upon me let this iniquity be: and let thine handmaid, I pray thee, speak in thine audience, and hear the words of thine handmaid. Let not my lord, I pray thee, regard this man of Belial, even Nabal: for as his name is, so is he; Nabal is his name, and folly is with him: but I thine handmaid saw not the young men of my lord, whom thou didst send. Now therefore, my lord, as the Lord liveth, and as thy soul liveth, seeing the Lord hath withholden thee from coming to shed blood, and from avenging thyself with thine own hand, now let thine enemies, and they that seek evil to my lord, be as Nabal. And now this blessing which thine handmaid hath brought unto my lord, let it even be given unto the young men that follow my lord. I pray thee, forgive the trespass of thine handmaid: for the Lord will certainly make my lord a sure house; because my lord fighteth the battles of the Lord, and evil hath not been found in thee all thy days. Yet a man is risen to pursue thee, and to seek thy soul: but the soul of my lord shall be bound in the bundle of life with the Lord thy God; and the souls of thine enemies, them shall he sling out, as out of the middle of a sling. And it shall come to pass, when the Lord shall have done to my lord according to all the good that he hath spoken concerning thee, and shall have appointed thee ruler over Israel; That this shall be no grief unto thee, nor offence of heart unto my lord, either that thou hast shed blood causeless, or that my lord hath avenged himself: but when the Lord shall have dealt well with my lord, then remember thine handmaid."*

Listen very carefully, please, and catch the wisdom this woman used to avert a bloodbath, saving the lives of her husband, her servants, herself, and David's men, and protecting the anointing and the call on David's life. The very first thing she said to David was to let him know that if there was any problem between him and Nabal, then let the problem fall on her. She was saying, "Go ahead and avenge yourself by killing me. It's fine with me. I'm willing to give up my life to protect his." If that is not true love and humility, I don't know what is. What a husband and a real man should have done for his wife was what Abigail was doing for Nabal.

Immediately after humbling herself, Abigail requested to speak to David, not as the heiress to all the property that Nabal owned, but to speak to David as a servant, and ask to be heard. Abigail did not force herself, assume, or demand to be heard. She negotiated with David with honor, respect, authority, and humility. I say authority because she was in a position of power, and she commanded that authority by her actions and behavior. You see, you can humble yourself even as the chief executive officer of any company. Blessings follow when it is done properly and in order, as we see in this story.

Abigail was not naïve to Nabal's foolish behaviors. She admits it right up front, calling her husband a fool before another man did. Let me put what she said in our language: "Had I known your men came to see us, I would have handled everything from there, but my husband was the one your men talked to. Because they talked to him, I had no knowledge of what had transpired until after he acted like a fool, living up to his name." Take cautious notice; she calls her husband a fool before David and his six hundred men, reminding everyone that she wasn't being disrespectful to her husband; rather, she acknowledged that his behavior equaled his name. How brilliant that was!

Acknowledging the mistake, the foolishness, the stupidity, and the wickedness of her husband was the first thing David and his men needed to hear. Now she was in a position where she could actually change the outcome of the situation at hand. Then she reminded him that God lives, and God lived within him, protected him, and held him back from moving forward with his plan, which would have led to bloodshed. How would God have held David back? He held him back when the entourage of donkeys arrived with food and drink, meeting every need those men had. God made the provision. Notice carefully how Abigail never said, "I gave you the food." This woman would be my best friend if she were alive today. She took no credit for her ingenuity at this point. She then reminded him to allow God to defend him. After all, God did not need Nabal to provide for David and his men. Abigail continued to tell David to let God take care of his enemies, all those who would oppose him, and those who were like Nabal. Isn't that interesting? Did Abigail know the destiny of her husband? I don't know if she did or not, but she, being a godly woman, knew that her husband's future was sealed.

Please pay attention to what I'm about to say next. She came in for the kill. Up until then, Abigail had not taken credit for bringing the food. The reasons why were, first, she needed to establish that it was God who made the provision. Now she was reminding him that God used her to bring it to him, and not only to him but there was so much food and drink that he could also share with all of those men who blessed him. Do you see what she did here? She gave glory to God for the provision and then let them know how God deserved the glory for how He provided. She acknowledged that God used her to bring about peace, the very peace that David had initially brought Nabal but Nabal rejected. David talked about peace, but Abigail brought "the peace offering." I say the "peace offering" because she told David that his anger could fall upon her right away. David and four hundred of his men were set to kill and murder Nabal, her, and their household. Here you see beautifully displayed and brilliantly executed that she sent the food first. She was now able to lay down the groundwork of her presentation. She asked David to please forgive her for the offense. I am in awe of this statement. She took the fault for her husband's offense, even though she did nothing wrong. David and those men knew it, too. You see, this is what a good wife does.

Abigail guarded her husband by taking the blame for his actions onto herself. Let me tell you why this is so important. In doing this, she diverted all of that anger from a man who actually did deserve it and she diffused the situation. There is an Italian proverb that my mother used all the time when I was growing up when my brothers and I were fighting, "Don't light your match. When you see fire on the ground, you don't light your match. It is the only way you don't cause an explosion." It is clear to understand the Italian proverb my mother used. You don't add your own match to a wildfire. You diffuse it. You come up with ways to stop the fire from spreading. This is exactly what Abigail did. She protected her husband by saying it was her fault. Anyone with half of a brain would have understood that she didn't know anything about it until after the fact. When she did know something about it, she immediately made the provisions. David, who was enraged, would understand what just took place, and therefore, she diffused the fire. You see her wisdom in full display. In the same sentence, she affirmed him by telling him certainly God would make him a sure house because David fought the battles of the Lord. If that was not enough, she reminded him that evil was not to be found in him, not today or any day of his life. What a prophetic statement! David was not used to people speaking life into him. David was used to being betrayed, rejected, and thought low of by people, including his family, especially his wife, Michal.

Suddenly, this woman came, a total stranger, humbling herself and reminding David of who he was in God, chosen and appointed by God. In the capacity of a peacemaker, Abigail chose her words carefully to remind David of the great destiny and future God had for him. Anything he did in the heat of anger would cause him harm and cost him future blessings. Nabal's response to David was insolent, debilitating, and filled with malice. The greeting and response Abigail gave to David was like a spring gushing fresh, clean water out of nowhere. Her words resurrected peace within David, revived him, and calmed him down from his anger.

The last statement she made to David is vital. You cannot miss the power of her final statement. Out of nowhere, found in Samuel 25:30 (KJV), she said, *"And it shall come to pass, when the Lord shall have done to my lord according to all the good that he hath spoken concerning thee, and shall have appointed thee ruler over Israel..."* Did you catch that? How did she know that God had spoken to him concerning his future and that He had anointed David to be the next ruler of Israel? Nobody knew that except David, his family, and Samuel, who anointed him. Let me tell you how: God brought to David a prophetic word to remind him who he was to be. God had not ordered David to go kill Nabal. Again, as Abigail stated earlier on, God kept David from shedding blood unnecessarily. You see, God had a plan in place already. The plan was Abigail. She was not sent just to bring him physical food but to feed him spiritually. The Bible does not say Abigail was a prophetess, but I believe it is safe to say that Abigail gave a prophetic word in this verse we see in 1 Samuel 25:30. David knew it to be true because God already told him through the prophet Samuel. Can you picture the stunned look on David's face? He had to accept the provision that God made for him and his men from the hand of Abigail. Not only the physical provision, but also the spiritual provision for David's soul, noted in 1 Samuel 25:29 (KJV), which says, *"Yet a man is risen to pursue thee, and to seek thy soul: but the soul of my lord shall be bound in the bundle of life with the Lord thy God; and the souls of thine enemies, them shall he sling out, as out of the middle of a sling."*

God was about to avenge David and would smite his enemy. That privilege and honor belonged to God, not David. Did you clearly understand this? Our enemies are God's enemies. They will never prevent us nor stop us from fulfilling God's perfect plans and purposes for our lives. He will remove our enemies however He sees fit.

In conclusion to her speech, she made a bold statement. We see her statement in 1 Samuel 25:31 (KJV), *"...but when the Lord shall have dealt well with my lord, then remember thine handmaid."* She made a bold, confident, and courageous petition. She was absolutely fearless. Up until this point, neither David nor the men uttered one word. She had the ear of the future king, and she knew it. Oh, the power of positive words! Oh, the power of anointed words! Abigail covered all her points. She was concise and thorough, and she left no detail out. That speech was never forgotten by David. Talk about leaving an everlasting impression. It is not the way you look that leaves an impression. It is your words. Once words are spoken, they can never be taken back. Her words, along with her actions, changed both of their destinies.

We find what David said to Abigail in 1 Samuel 25:32-35 (KJV), *"And David said to Abigail, Blessed be the Lord God of Israel, which sent thee this day to meet me: And blessed be thy advice, and blessed be thou, which hast kept me this day from coming to shed blood, and from avenging myself with mine own hand. For in very deed, as the Lord God of Israel liveth, which hath kept me back from hurting thee, except thou hadst hasted and come to meet me, surely there had not been left unto Nabal by the morning light any that pisseth against the wall. So David received of her hand that which she had brought him, and said unto her, Go up in peace to thine house; see, I have hearkened to thy voice, and have accepted thy person."* I am amazed that David touched on all of Abigail's points in her speech with so few words. First, he blessed everything she said. With every point he made he said the word "blessed." In plain old English, this is what he was saying, "You are redeemed. You are rewarded. You are saved. All because I recognize that you are spiritual in the ways and laws of the Lord. You hold the Word of God to be sacred. Because your soul belongs to the living God, your beauty flows from the inside out and the Lord your God has exalted you." That's my interpretation, but in keeping with honesty, isn't that what David said to Abigail? He recognized who she was: a real woman of God; therefore, he took her advice, affirming to her what he was about to do in full detail. David demonstrated his gratefulness to Abigail by his actions. He listened to her very carefully, and he told her that he would do as she said. She could go in peace and know that David had listened to her and accepted the peace offering and all she had to say. What a dramatic ending to a potentially disastrous and deadly situation.

After a successful negotiation, Abigail mounted her donkey. She returned home with her entourage only to find a drunk husband along with the entire household. I want to pause here and point out a very significant and truthful statement. Can you imagine the bloodbath that would have occurred if David and his men were not stopped? Nabal and his servants were so drunk they wouldn't have known what hit them. They and their children, along with their wives, would have been slaughtered.

Those men were not in the right kind of mind or fit to defend themselves, never mind their wives and children. What a terrible position they would have been in. Hands-down, David and his men would have won. Have you ever seen a drunk person? They cannot even touch their nose or stay balanced. How would they have been able to fight off David and his men? Abigail was a heroine! God used this godly woman to save the lives of her household, including her and her foolish husband. Obviously, I am not a fan of Nabal. His ungodly and wicked ways put his life in danger and that of his wife and entire household.

What happens next is quick and swift. Abigail had just told David the day before that God would smite his enemies. Now, she told her husband why she was missing and not at his feast fit for kings. The man had a heart attack right then and there. Reality set in: "Hey, I was almost killed." Please do not think that he had concern for his wife or household. His household clearly showed that he was rude, ungodly, and condescending to David. Ten days later, Nabal died. What a sad ending for Nabal.

Here's the truth: it didn't have to go down that way. Nabal could have humbled himself and made things right before his wife and David, but God knows the heart and its intentions. God knew this man would never leave his foolishness. I believe that God honored Abigail for what she did to save the future king. Remember that David had just blessed her for everything she had done. God was way ahead of David. He was about to reward her by making her a queen, and she didn't even know it.

This story ends beautifully. Immediately after Abigail's time of mourning was done, David sent his men for her hand in marriage. David wasted no time in making her his wife. He had come to take her away quickly the next day after the last day of mourning.

In conclusion, we end this amazing story of a very courageous and godly woman. In the end, because she did what was righteous in the eyes of God, as a result, God honored her for her godly behavior and elevated her to be the wife of David, soon to be Queen Abigail. What an ending! God removed Nabal, a wicked and foolish husband, and gave her David, a godly and wise husband.

Righteous living always wins in the end.

Study Guide

As we see in the story of Abigail, she truly was a woman of good understanding. She also did what was right, and she was blessed. She demonstrated this Bible verse found in Psalm 106:3 (KJV) very well: *"Blessed are they that keep judgment, and he that doeth righteousness at all times."* Nabal, a fool by name and character, was an ungodly man. He treated King David disrespectfully with an insolent response that would bring bloodshed to his home. However, when she found out how Nabal had treated King David, Abigail quickly jumped into action, wasting no time, saving the lives of her husband, her servants, herself, and David's men, and protecting the anointing call on David's life. She did what was honorable and right, and as a result, everyone and everything on their property was saved.

1. Who was Nabal? What lineage was he from? Why is his lineage so significant?

2. Think about and discuss King David's greeting versus Nabal's response; why was Nabal's response uncalled-for and insolent?

3. Was King David's reaction to Nabal's response right or wrong? Explain.

4. When Abigail found out about how Nabal responded to King David, what did Abigail do?

5. What was Abigail trying to prevent? Explain why it was important for Abigail to approach King David in the manner that she did.

CHAPTER 4
LIVE YOUR LIFE
PART 2

Bathsheba

In this story, contrary to Abigail's wise and godly behavior, we find an ungodly woman who used poor judgment and caused the downfall of King David. There is a lesson that needs to be made very clear. King David and Bathsheba participated consensually and willingly in this act of sexual sin. They did not understand, nor could they have foreseen the consequences that would run through King David's family from the moment they committed the act right on into the future. The sword never left King David's household. King David and Bathsheba's sin affected them, but it also affected everyone around them, including their children. The results of their sin were lasting, and King David's greatness had been snuffed out, all because Bathsheba did not take the same position as the godly Abigail.

The story of Bathsheba and David is truly a sad one. Let me explain why. David was a man who had been anointed by

Almighty God to become King of Israel. Literally, the hand of God was upon him. The trials and tribulations he encountered since the time Samuel anointed him were astonishing. Yet the hand of God never departed from him. This is why I say we come to a time in his life where he committed the greatest of sins. At this point in time, David would have been in his fifties with wives and concubines. As king, he could have had any single woman regardless of age. Instead, he chose a married woman, but not just any married woman.

King David was disrespectful to those who were loyal to him and served him very well. In David's army, Bathsheba's father, Eliam, was a mighty man. Her grandfather, Ahithophel, was one of King David's chief counselors. Furthermore, she married Uriah the Hittite, another mighty man in his army. King David knew this information before he had her come to him.

Let's pick up the story here in 2 Samuel 11:2 (KJV), *"And it came to pass in an eveningtide, that David arose from off his bed, and walked upon the roof of the king's house: and from the roof he saw a woman washing herself; and the woman was very beautiful to look upon."* Here, the key point is that King David was out of line. He couldn't sleep because he was supposed to be at war, commanding his army. Because he was not where he was supposed to be, he got himself into trouble. He chose to stay behind for no good reason. Satan took advantage of the fact that King David was out of the will of God. Satan has the upper hand whenever we are not where we are supposed to be.

In this case, the Word of God says he was pacing back and forth, undoubtedly because he was worried about how the war was going. Had he been at war commanding the army, he wouldn't have been restless and on top of his roof watching a woman purifying herself. Now let me just say that I am not a fan of Bathsheba. Bathsheba is definitely not my role model. However, I do not feel it is right to speak ill of her without completely understanding this story.

Despite popular belief, Bathsheba did not go to the rooftop to seduce the King. She had no idea that the King was watching her. In fact, she was likely in the mikvah, a naturally collected or flowing water bath used for the ceremonial cleansing and purification immersion ritual that Jewish women take part in after their menstrual cycle. Today, these baths are very private. There can be nothing between the person and the water during this ritual. This includes clothing, jewelry, makeup, nail polish, hair strands, dirt, etc. Another woman with you makes sure that you are clean of such obstructions before you go in and that each submersion is complete. I want to clarify that Bathsheba, in no way, fashion, form, or shape, went to the rooftop to entice the King or any other man.

We need to ask: what was David doing on the roof of the king's house, to begin with? The Bible says he was lying in his bed and couldn't sleep. So, he got up and went to the roof. Let me tell you something very strongly. Every time you remove yourself from the perfect will of God, you get yourself in trouble, and we can see that here with King David. King David, the army commander-in-chief, was home instead of being at war with his troops. All the men who were of fighting age were at war. Therefore, King David was supposed to be with them, but he decided to stay behind. Why would he stay behind? All of his colleagues would have been at war. Now, King David found himself in a situation that led to lust, coveting, lying, adultery, and murder. Please understand, idleness is not a godly virtue. Idleness puts you at a disadvantage and in a place where you can be tempted. This is what King David put himself in. He saw beautiful Bathsheba, and immediately he asked who she was. King David's aid told him that the woman was Bathsheba and that she was Uriah the Hittite's wife. She wasn't married to just anyone; Uriah was a man of great valor and one of the mightiest warriors in King David's army. You would think that King David would have stopped there, having just found out she was married. Being a Jew himself, King David would have understood what Bathsheba was doing in the ceremonial place. However, what is seen through the eye is very powerful. He allowed himself to watch and entertain those lustful thoughts. In doing so, he began a spiral of destruction. He already knew she was doing a mikvah. Let's look to what happens next: King David ignored the fact that she was married to one of his soldiers; he sent men to her home and summoned her. Imagine this scene.

There is a knock on Bathsheba's door. She opens the door and is startled by the King's officers. She thinks immediately, "Did something happen to my husband?" Before she can say anything, they say, "King David has summoned you. Come with us." She hurriedly goes with the men, thinking, "Is my husband Uriah wounded? Is he dead? God, please don't let me hear bad news." Her heart is pounding with each step she takes. Every motion of horror and stress is aroused. She is terrified of what she might hear about her husband. She can hear her footsteps and the steps of the soldiers as they are going to the palace. She pictures herself kneeling before the King as he would be sitting on his throne, remembering all the Chief Counselor, her grandfather, had said about King David, about his kindness and his reverence and love for God. Suddenly, she doesn't find herself in the throne room, but she finds herself in his chambers, in other words, in the King's bedroom. Bathsheba, just like a lamb led to be slaughtered, went unaware of why the King summoned her. The woman had no clue what was about to happen to her, unlike Abigail, who knew ahead of the game that King David was about to murder her husband, her, and her household. I would like to mention that I understand why Bathsheba went to see King David up to this point. She had no idea that he wanted to commit adultery.

I want to point out that nowhere in the Bible makes the accusation that King David was a womanizer. Although the Bible does not approve of more than one wife, it was accepted behavior by people of old, especially kings. It would be understandable why Bathsheba would go with the men to King David, knowing that he was appointed and anointed by Jehovah God Himself. Remember, her grandfather was King David's chief counselor. Surely, if this was a habit of King David, her grandfather would have known this, and so would have Bathsheba. Up to this point, Bathsheba had done nothing wrong. Also, she knew David had seven wives already: Michal, Ahinoam, Abigail, Maacah, Haggith, Abital, and Eglah. She was married. She couldn't have thought that she was being summoned to have an affair.

Now everything changes, and this is where I start to hold her accountable. She, first, would have found out Uriah was fine. Nothing was wrong with Uriah. Business was conducted in the throne room, not the bedroom. However, Bathsheba was summoned to King David's private chambers. Like we would set the mood for an intimate time with our spouse, King David had set everything up for an adulterous affair. And this is what happens next, *"And David sent messengers, and took her; and she came in unto him, and he lay with her; for she was purified from her uncleanness: and she returned unto her house,"* (2 Samuel 11:4 KJV). Bathsheba could no longer deny what was before her eyes, and she had full knowledge of what King David was looking for. How foolish of Bathsheba.

Bathsheba was a woman of good character and moral standards until this moment. Here is where I begin to think differently about her. Some believe that King David raped her, but this is 100% incorrect. Neither the Bible nor the Hebrew manuscript call this rape. If King David had raped her, we would have known through the prophet Nathan, who confronted King David later on. In addition, we find rape mentioned two more times in the Bible, once with Amnon, David's son, and Dinah, Jacob's daughter. If King David had raped Bathsheba, it would have been mentioned in the story. King David did not force himself on Bathsheba to rape her. It was consensual, lustful, self-serving sex.

The Bible, in this story, does not provide any other explanation of what took place. Still, we understand a discussion would have taken place romantically and sexually because the Bible clearly says she laid with him. Did you catch that? She laid with him. At this point, Bathsheba brought disaster upon herself, upon her family, upon King David, upon the throne, upon his family, and upon the nation. What a difference between her actions and those of Abigail. Unrighteous behavior always brings destruction.

This is where Bathsheba made a serious error in judgment and sinned. One could say Bathsheba was afraid for her life or that the King could have caused trouble for her and Uriah. Some could say that she was powerless in the hands of a ruthless man. I'm sorry to say she sinned. Again, I am reminding the reader of who her father was, her grandfather, and her husband. She would have known it if King David was so ruthless and murderous. Up to this point, no stories were going around that he was this sinful, evil, or immoral man. We can, however, say he married ungodly women who bore him children who caused him nothing but grief, embarrassment, and shame. Outside of Abigail, he inherited Michal, who betrayed him by marrying another man. Even though King David took her back, she despised him, which caused a separation between the two. He inherited Ahinoam, who was King Saul's wife. In those days, that is what took place.

It was only years earlier that another woman, Abigail, had another kind of confrontation with King David. He had a murderous spirit, ready to annihilate Abigail, her husband Nabal, and her household. As we read about it earlier, Abigail, filled with godly wisdom, character, and integrity was able to turn the heart of King David to not commit such an evil act before a holy and righteous God. She threw herself at his mercy, not caring about her life. As we already discovered, Abigail was a woman of holiness, and it showed in her character and behavior.

It is necessary to point out that fear for your life does not excuse you from obeying God. It is necessary to know that back in King David's day, you just didn't refuse the request of any king without fear of losing your life. We find Queen Esther standing up before King Artaxerxes. Her head and her life were in danger as well. However, she did what was right before God, and God protected her.

Please understand, we are not saying Bathsheba did not have a choice. She had a choice to refuse King David or not. If she said no, she would risk the possibility of being killed. There are several questions to consider if you were Bathsheba in this situation: could you imagine the amount of hurt your spouse would go through if you chose to commit adultery? What would be the consequences of your actions? Also, and most importantly, is a momentary illicit affair worth your relationship with God? Is it worth displeasing God for a few fleeting moments of committing the act of adultery that would have lasting effects on you and your children?

I can't help but think of another situation like Bathsheba's and how the person chose to handle it. Remember Joseph? Potiphar's wife wanted him. She wanted to have sex with him. Joseph said, "How could I do this evil before God?" Then, he ran from her presence. That woman accused him of rape and landed him in jail. He had no problem whatsoever about doing what was right before the throne room of God. It meant heads off with him, too. He chose the godly choice, and God delivered him. The reason for Bathsheba being so easily enticed is because it was a king who was flattering her. For a moment, she allowed herself to be seduced by his advances. She didn't run away like Joseph.

This is the reason why I brought in Abigail. Believe it or not, Abigail was also faced with the possibility of being killed. Still, because she was filled with the spirit of God, she used godly wisdom and protected King David. Bathsheba had a chance to throw herself at the mercy of King David once she knew why she had been summoned. Let me explain: King David took the advice of Abigail years earlier and didn't go through with his murderous plan. As a matter of fact, because Abigail had thrown herself at his mercy, he blessed her for keeping him from sinning. Bathsheba would have known about the sin of adultery. She would have known about the story of Joseph and how he kept himself from committing adultery. Bathsheba also knew God's law, which made her accountable before God for her sins. You would think Bathsheba wanted to keep her good reputation and her above-reproach character. She was the wife of a mighty soldier in the army. As we discussed already, she was a well-known and good God-fearing woman, not to mention her family lineage.

This was enough for her to have stopped anything from going further. If that didn't work, she should have realized God would not let them get away with their sin. So, when she was summoned, rather than taking a stand for the God she served, she, with King David's advances and request, complied and readily had sex with him. In that act, she became his accomplice in the sin of adultery. I want to make an important note here as well. Both King David and Bathsheba knew the great possibility of her conceiving a child. It is mentioned in the beginning that she was purifying herself, as stated in verse 4, *"...for she was purified from her uncleanness..."* What a contrast between Abigail and Bathsheba!

Whenever we are filled with the Spirit of God, we will make godly and righteous decisions, and it will be showcased by our actions. Clearly, we see a woman who allowed herself to become defiled in this story. So, I ask, what would have been the outcome if she had conducted herself in a godly manner? Here's what I believe would have happened. The avalanche that she set in motion would never have begun. In other words, King David would have let her go. Her husband would not have been murdered by her lover. She would never have conceived and given birth to a son whom God took after three days after delivery. King David would not have been punished by God by the worst kind of curse, *"The sword will never leave your home."* Ruin was brought to King David because she agreed to be a participant in the sin of adultery. Bathsheba remained as one of King David's wives. However, after all of this, we can find no mention of King David loving her. For example, we can discover where Jacob loved Rachel and Isaac loved Rebekah. Even in the story of Queen Esther, we can see where it says King Artaxerxes loved Queen Esther. Where can we find it telling that King David loved Bathsheba? Nowhere. That speaks volumes.

Ladies and Gentlemen, remember this truth: God will never condone, conceal, or justify sin. Just as King David and Bathsheba's sins found them out, so will any sin we commit find us out. In this story, the only righteous person was Uriah, Bathsheba's husband. What a sad turn of events.

The penalty for King David sinning caused an unwanted pregnancy, the murder of a godly man, making Joab an accomplice to the murder of Uriah, and the loss of his and Bathsheba's baby. In addition, the sword never left his house. His daughter, Tamar, was raped by his son, Amnon, which led to Absalom going after Amnon in vengeance for his sister, and Absalom then murdered Amnon. Absalom then led a civil war. Absalom then tried to steal the throne. Then, Absalom ended up dead.

Solomon, the son of David and Bathsheba, led the nation of Israel into sin because he married foreign wives who turned his heart away from the true living God.

Living a life of righteousness is attainable. It requires a heart sold out to God and a determination that you will not sin and cause God sorrow or cause disaster upon your life. Remember, Jesus was fully man and sinned not. We have a choice to either uphold the Ten Commandments or break them. That choice is up to us. I say walk in righteousness and obtain the favor of God and the blessings that come with it. Ladies, be an Abigail, and gentlemen, be a Uriah.

Study Guide

As we see in the story of Bathsheba, *"every one of us shall give account of himself to God, (Romans 14:12 KJV)."* Like Bathsheba was held accountable, we are held responsible for the choices we make as well. At some point in time, we have to decide to do things our way or God's way. Doing things our way will bring about disastrous consequences. It is always important to remember that your sin doesn't just affect you, but it also affects those around you. Bathsheba found herself at a crossroads. She could have stood up for what was right, done the courageous thing, and told King David as Joseph said to Potiphar's wife, "How then can I do this great wickedness *and sin against God?*" However, Bathsheba chose to do what was evil in the sight of God. The consequences of her actions could not be overturned; the sin of adultery she committed with King David affected her life, his life, and the lives of their families.

1. What are several questions that you should ask yourself if you find yourself at a crossroads like Bathsheba was when she was brought to King David's chambers?

2. Did Bathsheba have a choice as to whether or not she would participate in adultery, and how was it possible for Bathsheba to consent to commit an act of adultery? Explain.

3. Keeping in mind the story of Bathsheba, read 1 Corinthians 3:16-17 (KJV). *"Know ye not that ye are the temple of God, and that the Spirit of God dwelleth in you? If any man defile the temple of God, him shall God destroy; for the temple of God is holy, which temple ye are."* Remembering the story of Bathsheba, what does this Bible verse mean to you in looking at the story of Bathsheba? How did she and King David defile the temple of God? What laws of God did they break?

4. 2 Samuel 2:10 says, *"Now therefore the sword shall never depart from your house; because you have despised me..."* What is the significance of that verse, and what were some of the events that showed the truth of that verse?

5. What does the story of Bathsheba show us about unrighteous living?

CHAPTER 5
DON'T GIVE UP
PART 1

Caleb

Caleb was an amazing man, and the Hebrew meaning of his name completely describes this great and righteous man of God. The Hebrew spelling of Caleb's name is "Kelev," which means "dog." The name Caleb, in Hebrew, is a compound word. Since that is the basis for this word, one can take note that the other meaning for this word, "Kelev," is "faithful, devoted, wholehearted, bold, brave." This is not uncommon, and it is quite a phenomenon in Ancient Hebrew. That meaning describes Caleb perfectly.

Let's take a good look at this righteous man of God. You can read the whole story of Caleb's early years in Numbers 13 and 14. We are going to touch upon some of these verses. We first hear about Caleb in Numbers 13 when God told Moses to send men out to spy out the land of Canaan, *"And the Lord spake unto Moses, saying, Send thou men, that they may search the land of*

Canaan, which I give unto the children of Israel: of every tribe of their fathers shall ye send a man, every one a ruler among them," (Numbers 13:1-2 KJV).

Moses had chosen one spy from each tribe. Caleb was chosen to represent the tribe of Judah. Everyone knew God had told them through Moses that God Himself was giving them the land of Canaan. This promise from God should have been enough. They had God's word. God never instructed them to spy out the land. He said, *"Go and possess the land that I am going to give you."* Not only did God tell them to possess the land, He told them which land to possess, the land of Canaan; what they would find in Canaan was a land flowing with milk and honey. You see, what should have happened didn't take place. They should have immediately taken possession of the land. After all, they had seen how God had worked for them in taking other places. You would think that they would have happily marched forward with great shouts of joy. However, that is not what happened. They foolishly went out and spied out the land. They went everywhere. They saw clusters of grapes being carried between two men on a pole. They saw giants in the land, descendants of Anak. Their hearts became frightened, and faith went out the door.

The interesting thing about all of this is that God allowed their stiff-necked approach to spy out the land for forty days. I want to point out something very important here. Throughout the Bible, when God wanted to test His people, He used forty days or forty years to do so. In the spies' forty days of investigation, God was doing the looking. That looking was at their hearts. Their hearts did not contain faith, trust, or the belief that God was about to give them the land they saw with their own eyes flowing with milk and honey. All they saw were men who were giants and the fruit that were giants as well. Whenever we do not act on what God tells us to do, all we see are the gigantic mountains that stand in our way. They were filled with trembling fear, bringing that back to the camp. All they could talk about was how they could not beat the obstacles in their way. How sad is that? All the people could do was concentrate on the bad report and not on the specific promise of God. Now they had failed the test completely. Do you understand why I said they foolishly went out to spy on the land? God never told them to spy out the land. He told them to go and possess the land.

Thank God that Caleb objected along with Joshua. Caleb quieted the people, and he did this right before Moses. *"And Caleb stilled the people before Moses, and said, Let us go up at once, and possess it; for we are well able to overcome it,"* (Numbers 13:30 KJV). Did you catch that? Caleb lived up to the meaning of his name "bold and brave," commanded the people, and was quick to trust and obey God. He reminded them that they needed to take the land because it wasn't the people who would fight on their behalf but God Himself. He was courageous. Not only did he want them to go possess the land, but he wanted to go now, immediately, just as God commanded. It took a lot of courage amid doubtful and unbelieving people. Go, Caleb, go! However, the other spies were not seeing it from a spiritual perspective. Up until this point, coming from Egypt, nothing was normal. Nothing they saw was normal. Everything God did was supernatural, unbelievable, and unexplainable by man's human reasoning.

You would think they would have understood when God said to go to Canaan because He would give them possession of that land. Instead, they allowed unbelief to make them cower and keep them from the blessing. You see, unbelief is very dangerous. Many times, unbelief shows itself in reason and in rationale. However, when it comes to obeying God's command, reason and logic go out the window. You must do what God tells you to do, and what He tells you to do may not sound logical or reasonable to you or anyone else. The fact is that the children of God live by faith because it is impossible to please Him without faith. All we should do is trust the Word of God. Remember this, when God says "GO," you go. Don't discourage yourself by imagining all the possible scenarios, all the "if's," and all the "buts." Just do what God told you to do. This is how you possess the miracles and blessings.

Caleb was nothing like the ten evil spies. I say evil because they went against the Word of God, the actual command to go in and possess the land of Canaan. It was a direct defiance, and it started when they decided to go and spy it out to see if they could or could not conquer it. This had nothing to do with them. They, on their own, could do nothing. This was about God and His miraculous fulfillment of taking them out of Egypt and bringing them to their own land. Did they forget the ten plagues God brought on Egypt so that they could be released? They saw rivers and seas and every pot and pool filled with blood. They saw frogs everywhere. Let's not forget the swarms of locust all over the land. Then there was the first child of every Egyptian family dying because they didn't have the blood on their doorposts. All those plagues never touched the Israelites; they only touched the Egyptians. That alone should have shown God's power to them. Finally, they saw the parting of the Red Sea and walked on dry land, and then once they were across, they began to see the water cover and flood the entire Egyptian army. Wasn't that more than enough for them to know and believe God would protect them and give them the land that He promised them? Listen very carefully. Whenever you decide to defy God, you forfeit His blessings. The righteous live by faith. Caleb was a righteous man. The ten unbelieving spies brought sin into their camp by convincing people to disbelieve God. It didn't matter what Caleb and Joshua had to say. They were crippled by fear. I wonder what would have happened if they had obeyed God without going to check it out first. Today, people do that, too. When God tells us to do something, we often try to reason our way out of it, or we try to understand what He wants by human logic. It doesn't work that way. Again, the righteous live by faith. As we continue to see in this story, God's anger is showcased by telling them that none of them, except for Caleb and Joshua, would see the Promised Land. God honored their faithfulness and obedience to Him. They just had to wait until the rest of their generation died before they would see the Promised Land again.

Let's fast forward forty-five years later. Caleb was eighty-five years old, and he not only conquered the land but also took the biggest mountain called Mount Hebron. Look at what God does for the righteous, and in this case, Caleb. The other ten spies paralyzed themselves and all of Israel with fear. The sin they committed was so great before the eyes of God: the sin of unbelief. It is a huge offense to God because when we do not believe Him, we are calling Him a liar. God is not a man that He should lie and not a man that He should change His mind. We cannot put God on the same level as man and think that we will get away with it. He who promised can perform it. What's even worse is that they brought unbelief to an entire nation. The people demanded spies, and they got what they wanted. They got a bad report. They started this whole thing with fear and unbelief, and God tested them by allowing ten out of the twelve spies to come back and tell them what they saw. The truth is that had they gone to war with the spirit of unbelief, they would have been slaughtered. Oh, the power of unbelief and the destruction it causes! They lost the right to enter and possess the Promised Land because of their unbelief. That was the penalty God rendered unto them for their wrongdoing. In the process, they lost their property, home, and inheritance. God did not allow them the privilege of settling down into their own home. They died in the wilderness. That is the portion of the sin of rebellion and unbelief for unrighteous living.

Caleb, on the other hand, not only inherited the Promised Land, but he asked Joshua for the biggest mountain to conquer: *"Now therefore give me this mountain, whereof the Lord spake in that day; for thou heardest in that day how the Anakims were there, and that the cities were great and fenced: if so be the Lord will be with me, then I shall be able to drive them out, as the Lord said. And Joshua blessed him, and gave unto Caleb the son of Jephunneh Hebron for an inheritance,"* (Joshua 14:12-13 KJV).

Why on earth would Caleb want Mount Hebron? Why was this mountain so important to Caleb? Caleb still hung on to God's promise to His people to bring them into the Promised Land. Caleb never gave up. There was a promise made by God. He believed that promise. He believed the Lord would give His people the land. He tried to convince the Israelites and the rest of the ten spies. No one stood with him except Joshua. However, the dream and the promise never died within him. Forty-five years later, Caleb was just as passionate at the age of eighty-five as he was at the age of forty. He was ready, prepared, and determined to possess the land that the Lord had promised him. I want us to understand that he did not ask for just any portion of land; he asked specifically for Mount Hebron.

Do you see what I see? The people didn't want to go into Hebron because they feared the giants. However, Caleb knew what God had promised, and Caleb was going to take the land God had already given to them. He wasn't going to back down, be afraid, or forfeit what God said belonged to him. Friends, may I submit to you that Caleb did not just want any land but the land that God had promised. He wanted not just God's will, but he wanted God's perfect will for his life. Caleb wanted to show the people that with God, nothing was impossible. Giants or no giants, God would win.

The giants lived there, but he would slay them because God had already given them victory. He had his job, which was to believe God no matter how long it took, in this case, forty-five years, and when the time came, he had to act in faith. In other words, forty-five years earlier, he wanted to take possession of the land, but the people stopped him. He had no choice but to wait until God said "go" again. The time had come, and Caleb still had the fire burning inside of him to receive what God had promised.

Because Caleb was loyal to the promise and persistent in his actions, Joshua blessed him to receive his portion, but God brought it to completion. God honored Caleb. Caleb got the very land that God said was his inheritance. This is why we don't give up on the promises of God. Secondly, it's imperative to understand that it doesn't matter how old you are or what socio-economic status or gender you are, you are not to give up on the promises of God. Here we clearly see a man who was eighty-five years old and wanted the most difficult portion of land for his inheritance. He was so convinced that the Lord his God would be faithful to His promise to the Israelites that Caleb said, *"As yet I am as strong this day as I was in the day that Moses sent me: as my strength was then, even so is my strength now, for war, both to go out, and to come in."* Do you understand how powerful this statement is? Are there men out there today who are eighty-five years old, dressed for war and with the strength of a forty-year-old to go out and conquer the enemy? Not just any place anywhere in the battle but on the frontlines. This is what Mount Hebron represented: the toughest and the fiercest. Here is this eighty-five-year-old man filled with the power of God who led his army and conquered Mount Hebron. Do you understand that God was with him the entire time? There was no Israelite who wouldn't have seen the display of God's glory and power in this incredible takeover of land.

Thirdly, why did God want the Israelites to conquer Mount Hebron? Let's have a little bit of a history and geography lesson regarding this mountain. Hebron is located thirty-two kilometers south of Jerusalem. It's an interesting land because Mount Hebron is actually built on hills, and these hills contain channels. These channels are critical because they collect and hold the water in the rainy season. As we all know, water is essential to livestock and vegetation, not to mention necessary for drinking. The mountain contained everything. No wonder the giants took the best of the land. God's intention was to give His people the very best. They forfeited that forty-five years earlier. Caleb did not. I don't believe Caleb wanted Hebron because of the terrain. I know that for a fact. He said the reason why, which we have already discussed. My only reason for mentioning this type of land is to remind the reader that we are never to give up the best God wants to give us. In order to receive the best, there are times when you must step out in faith and act upon what God has promised, regardless of what or who stands in your way. Caleb no longer could wait. He had to act, and he did. He did not squander time. He stepped up and took what God told him was his. Interestingly enough, Hebron is where the patriarchs are buried, meaning Abraham and Sarah, Isaac and Rebecca, Jacob and Leah. No wonder God wanted to give them back the land where their own patriarchs were buried.

As I read this story, I cannot believe that the Israelites would have caved in and cowered, disobeying a direct command God had given them to go and possess what already belonged to them. Caleb regained the very territory that belonged to God's people. He regained the land by driving out the enemies living there as God had wanted them to do. He did a complete takeover. He left nothing undone. He followed God's instructions and drove the enemies off his possessed land.

Hebron represents something else, and I don't believe this is coincidental. Hebron means "friend" translated from the Hebrew word "chaver." Why don't we do a little calculation here? Abraham was called a friend of God, and Abraham was buried in Mount "Friend." God promised Abraham, His friend, that his descendants would be more than the stars in the sky and more than the grains of the sand. Wouldn't it make sense then for God to give the Israelites that particular place, that particular land? He was bringing them back to their roots. God calls His friends those who believe in Him and His promises. Abraham believed God, and so did Caleb. What a beautiful picture of Caleb looking at the mountain he conquered through the help of God and constantly being reminded that he, too, was a friend of God. Every time someone would ask Caleb, "What is your possession, Caleb?" The response would always be, "I live in Mount Friend." He knew that God, his friend, gave him the very best, reminding him that his entire faith was passed on from generation to generation. You can't go wrong when you choose to follow God. If you want to possess a promise God has given, you will have to live a life of right-eousness just as Caleb did.

To receive God's best for us, we must live a life of righteousness with our faith firmly planted in God without wavering so that we can conquer the land God has promised us as His friend.

Caleb, as we see in this story, fought for his inheritance. He would not let go of the land flowing with milk and honey. He was going to fight, conquer, regain, and possess the land God swore to give Abraham. He was not going to forfeit his inheri-tance. Righteous people never give up on the promises of God.

Study Guide

As we see in the story of Caleb, "...*the just shall live by his faith.*" Caleb was a man of extraordinary faith. Like Caleb, as children of the Most High God, we can trust God and take Him at His Word. We can learn a lot from Caleb. Caleb was righteous because he was a man of faith and acted in faith. He walked by faith and not by sight. He trusted the promises of God and did not waver in that faith. It wasn't until forty-five years later that

Caleb took hold of his possession, the Promised Land. Caleb conquered the Promised Land that the Israelites were afraid to go and possess due to their fear and lack of faith, knowing God had promised that land to His children long ago. He was victorious in conquering and taking over the land that was the inheritance of his people.

1. How did Caleb demonstrate that we, as the children of God, walk by faith and not by sight? Why was the good report that he brought back important?

2. How long did it take before Caleb could take possession of his inheritance, and why did it take so long for him to possess that land?

3. Why did Caleb want Mount Hebron? What was it about Mount Hebron that was special, and why was it desirable land?

4. What did Caleb want to show the Israelites?

5. Caleb was considered to be righteous. Why was he righteous? Based on Caleb's example of faithfulness, what is it that righteous people never do?

CHAPTER 6
DON'T GIVE UP
PART 2

Esau

The story of Esau is truly a sad one. God knits us together perfectly and forms our bodies in the shape and design that He likes, picking the color of our eyes, the shape of our nose, the texture and color of our hair, and the color of our skin. Still, there is something God will not do for us, which is to force us to have a heart that seeks after Him. This story should tell us very clearly that the Lord knows the intent of each heart before we are even born.

We must remember that God is all-knowing, always present, and all-powerful. There are things that our finite minds cannot fathom. We do not understand all mysteries of all things. At the time of our birth, God already knows what our heart is going to do. I find it very interesting that when these twins were in Rebekah's womb, God had already revealed their hearts, characters, and futures to her and to their father, Isaac.

Rebekah was having a difficult time conceiving. Isaac, the promised child to a woman who couldn't conceive, was a miracle child. He understood the promise God made his father that Abraham's descendants would be more numerous than the stars in the sky and the grains of sand on the ground. Isaac took control, believing the promise, and prayed for his wife Rebekah to conceive. God honored the prayer and kept that promise. Now Rebekah was pregnant and filled with great joy; she fully comprehended her call into this family of faith. She was one part of the grand design to multiply and fill the earth. Can you imagine when she felt all of this turmoil in her womb?

Let's imagine this scene. After such a long time of prayer and believing in God for Rebekah to become pregnant, suddenly, she conceived. This radiant and joyous woman was full of life and rejoicing in what God had done for her and Isaac. I can see her rubbing her belly, thanking God for the gift of a baby, wondering is this a boy or girl, what the baby will be like, what the baby will do, what the baby will look like, and all those things that a woman thinks and does when she is pregnant. I can imagine the love and tenderness given towards everything she did as she prepared for her delivery, sewing clothes and doing other things as they waited for the baby to arrive. Then, something strange began to happen. She felt a commotion going on in her womb, day in and day out. Not being able to fully understand what was going on inside of her, she decided to go enquire of the Lord. Let me just pause here for one second and make an important point. We, too, should be sensitive to what is happening around us. Too often, we run to spiritual leaders, family members, friends, and others to help us understand the turmoil that is going on within us. I'm not saying that you shouldn't do it or that it is a bad practice, but what I am suggesting is that we, too, be as quick as Rebekah to go enquire of the Lord. Only the Lord has the perfect answer for every struggle we go through. I believe Rebekah knew that whatever was going on in her womb was from the spiritual perspective. I say this because Rebekah was very well aware of how God matched her and Isaac together. It was a divine marital union. She also knew the mandate that was given to her father-in-law, Abraham. She knew of God's covenant with Abraham of Isaac being the sole heir. She also knew that for the promises of God to come to pass, she would have to bear children. Notice here in Genesis 25:22 (KJV) the wording, *"And the children struggled together within her..."* The Hebrew word for "struggled" is "rat-sas," which means "grievously oppressed, crushed." Did you catch that? Within herself, she felt grievously oppressed. She was literally in pain. Let me explain it to you this way. In her womb, those children were fighting, and it was as if they were crushing each other into pieces. Her womb was being literally crushed. She felt the pain. I guess only women who have been pregnant can understand this scenario. Please note that she didn't run to a midwife or whoever was part of her neighborhood who would have been in charge of delivering her baby.

I believe Rebekah knew what was happening inside of her was a spiritual matter and why she took it to the God who sees all things and knows all things, *"and she said, If it be so, why am I thus? And she went to enquire of the Lord,"* (Genesis 25:22 (KJV). Now we see Rebekah going before the presence of God, making her request, and waiting for God to answer. Suddenly, God revealed to her what was happening. Imagine the shock when she learned that she didn't have just one baby in her womb, but she had two. I'm sure double joy is the first thing she felt, especially Rebekah, who had difficulty getting pregnant. Now she heard the good news that God was blessing her with two babies. However, what she heard next was a game-changer. Let's look at what God said: *"And the Lord said unto her, Two nations are in thy womb, and two manner of people shall be separated from thy bowels; and the one people shall be stronger than the other people; and the elder shall serve the younger,"* (Genesis 25:23 (KJV). To hear *"the elder shall serve the younger"* would have been a shock to Rebekah and Isaac because culturally in ancient Israel, during this time, the eldest son was of the utmost importance and would have gained a significant portion of the inheritance. Upon the father's death, it would be the eldest son who would become the family's patriarch. This news went against the cultural belief system. To top everything off, she found out that she was pregnant with two nations.

God was preparing the hearts of Rebekah and Isaac for what their family would be dealing with. Each twin represented not just individual characters; each twin represented a nation: Jacob, who would later have his name changed to Israel, from whom the faithful line of God's people and the Messiah would come from, and Esau, who from the day he was born, was not just called Esau, but also Edom. Edom would be another country that would be an enemy nation of Israel. These two brothers would clash in every possible way. These two children were different in manners, dispositions, and attitudes, and it began within the womb. You see, the Word of God is very clear when God says, *"The heart is deceitful above all things, and desperately wicked: who can know it? I the LORD search the heart, I try the reins, even to give every man according to his ways, and according to the fruit of his doings,"* (Jeremiah 17:9-10 KJV). God knew Esau's heart, and He knew Jacob's heart before they came into existence. God knew Esau would not follow His ways and even despise his birthright. However, Jacob was the promised child, and Jacob would be the one who would follow the laws of God, carrying forth the faithful line that would bring forth the Messiah.

This word God spoke to Rebekah was concluded in 2 Chronicles 21:8 in the house of David when they revolted. You see, God was preparing the hearts of Rebekah and Isaac for what was to come. One child would serve God, and the other child would be rebellious. Imagine Rebekah's heart. She had the Word of God to confirm the future for what God called her for and the continuation of the future nation of what would become Israel. There is no mention of Rebekah arguing with God, no begging God to change His mind, no crying, no poor me; Rebekah was silent. She was so silent that she didn't share this information with anyone that we know of. We can speculate all we want; maybe she told Isaac, maybe she didn't. We don't know. If she had, we don't hear anything from Isaac regarding his feelings towards it. In fact, we don't hear anything more about whether Jacob and Esau continued to struggle in her or not. The next event is found in Genesis 25:24-25 (KJV), *"And when her days to be delivered were fulfilled, behold, there were twins in her womb. And the first came out red, all over like an hairy garment; and they called his name Esau. And after that came his brother out, and his hand took hold on Esau's heel; and his name was called Jacob: and Isaac was threescore years old when she bare them."*

When Esau and Jacob become adults, we start to clearly see the differences in attitudes and characters of these two brothers.

Esau was a hunter and very careless in his actions; Jacob was a quiet man who stayed among the tents while Esau hunted wild animals. We begin to see the true character of each of the twins.

I find it interesting that Jacob wanted the birthright. The birthright came with a lot of responsibilities, obligations, and honor. The firstborn would be in charge of all the property and the dispersing of any property if necessary to their siblings, continuing the legacy of this great family. It was the firstborn who received a double portion of the inheritance. God had spoken to Abraham and called Abraham out of Ur of Chaldea, bringing him into a land he did not know. During Abraham's journey, God was continually leading him, and God promised that he would be the father of many nations. Remember, it was Caleb who conquered the original inheritance which was promised to the children of Israel. Abraham was just the beginning of this legacy. The inheritance was to be passed on from generation to generation. The truth of the matter is, God had already chosen Jacob in his mother's womb to become the father of the twelve tribes of Israel. Because God knew the heart and the intentions of Esau, Esau was bent on living a life of ungodliness and unrighteousness. Let's look at what occurs next.

In Genesis 25:29-34 (KJV), it says, *"And Jacob sod pottage: and Esau came from the field, and he was faint: And Esau said to Jacob, Feed me, I pray thee, with that same red pottage; for I am faint: therefore was his name called Edom. And Jacob said, Sell me this day thy birthright. And Esau said, Behold, I am at the point to die: and what profit shall this birthright do to me? And Jacob said, Swear to me this day; and he sware unto him: and he sold his birthright unto Jacob. Then Jacob gave Esau bread and pottage of lentiles; and he did eat and drink, and rose up, and went his way: thus Esau despised his birthright."* The word "despised" is translated from the Hebrew word "bazah," which means "to despise, hold in contempt, disdain." Oh my goodness! I cannot believe that Esau, a miracle child born to a woman who could only conceive by the power of the living God and born to a father who himself was also a miracle child, could feel such hate for the calling God had on his life. Esau would have understood and known who his grandfather was. He would have seen with his own eyes the blessings that would be his because of a righteous and holy man like his grandfather. Esau knew well that those blessings belonged to him, especially since he was the firstborn. Instead of being grateful for the blessings he inherited and was living in it at that moment, he was filled with scorn and disrespect for the privilege, honor, and blessings that came to him as the firstborn. Let me tell you something that was not the portion God had for him or for anyone else God has created. His heart was overflowing with an abundance of contempt and disdain. How in the world can this be?

Let me answer it for you in plain old English: when a person decides in his heart and sets his mind on doing that which is evil, evil takes over, and he loses all of his good senses. Do you see what Esau did? So disgusting before the eyes of God, not to mention disrespectful, dishonoring, and ungrateful. He rejected the most beautiful blessing that anyone could ever receive. Esau rejected it, and Jacob embraced and coveted it. In this case, coveting the blessings of God is not a sin. If you truly want the blessings of God that you see in someone's life, then you're not sinning in coveting the blessings by jealousy, but rather by inspiration and determination to see the blessings that God has for you as an individual.

Let me help you understand what this Hebrew word "bazah" really means. Esau loathed the birthright. He detested the birthright. He abhorred the birthright. This birthright, given by the great, awesome, and loving God, was scoffed at and treated like trash. Esau was repelled by it. To make it even worse, he mocked it and sneered at it. He literally found his inheritance to be intolerable. Esau regarded his birthright with contempt and was filled with contempt for it. That's what the Word of God tells us regarding his feelings for the birthright, his God-given blessing. It is important to note that when God gives blessings, it is not done on our terms. God gives us blessings on His terms. We're the vessels to carry it out in obedience. You see, although he sold a holy and consecrated birthright that was given through a promise by God to his grandfather and his father, which blessings were supposed to fall upon his head and his hands, he sold his birthright for a bowl of lentils. However, I believe he had no intention of keeping the oath he made to Jacob. If it were so, he would not have gotten so angry and filled with enough hate to want to murder his brother Jacob. Do you understand the point about sin? There comes the point when you regret the sins you committed, and it's too late, as in this case. Consequences still must be paid.

Esau's heart continues to show up in his actions. Let's take a look at how far Esau went in his destruction. In Genesis 26:34 (KJV), it says, *"And Esau was forty years old when he took to wife Judith the daughter of Beeri the Hittite, and Bashemath the daughter of Elon the Hittite."* Do you see what he did? Talk about contempt, disrespect, and dishonor toward God. Esau had no respect, no admiration, or appreciation for his father or mother. He ultimately disappointed his parents, and they acknowledged that disappointment.

The difference between Isaac and Esau is a vital one. Both had gotten married at 40 years old. However, Isaac listened to and obeyed Abraham and had reverence for the laws of God. Isaac had respect for Abraham, and he knew that he had to marry someone who did not belong to the enemy nations. Now we have Esau, who married foreign wives of the enemy nations. To completely slap the face of his father, Esau went a step further and married a daughter of Ishmael. The latter was conceived by Hagar, Sarah's slave, the very child God had Abraham send away. *"When Esau saw that Isaac had blessed Jacob, and sent him away to Padanaram, to take him a wife from thence; and that as he blessed him he gave him a charge, saying, Thou shalt not take a wife of the daughters of Canaan; And that Jacob obeyed his father and his mother, and was gone to Padanaram; And Esau seeing that the daughters of Canaan pleased not Isaac his father; Then went Esau unto Ishmael, and took unto the wives which he had Mahalath the daughter of Ishmael Abraham's son, the sister of Nebajoth, to be his wife."* (Genesis 28:6-9 KJV).

Generations later, we see what God had to say about the tribes that Esau's wives came from and what God had to say about the descendants of Esau: *"When the Lord thy God shall bring thee into the land whither thou goest to possess it, and hath cast out many nations before thee, the Hittites, and the Girgashites, and the Amorites, and the Canaanites, and the Perizzites, and the Hivites, and the Jebusites, seven nations greater and mightier than thou; And when the Lord thy God shall deliver them before thee; thou shalt smite them, and utterly destroy them; thou shalt make no covenant with them, nor shew mercy unto them,"* (Deuteronomy 7:1-2 KJV). This verse clearly shows that God was not pleased with Esau's choice for wives. Be very careful whom you choose to make an unholy alliance with, whether it is a choice of spouse or friends.

Esau was bent on destroying the covenant God had made with Abraham. Please clearly understand, Esau's plan was already put in motion in his heart before he even came out. God already knew the state of Esau's heart and what Esau would choose to do. This indicates that without Christ and without repentance, we are capable of the most heinous crimes and acts. Whether we accept or reject Jesus Christ, our Lord, and Savior, the choice is ours.

You see, Esau married not just into one nation but into two nations, which were enemies of God. If Esau had received his birthright, he would have had to pass it down as an inheritance to his own children. His children would have been born from these wives he took to marry. Being part of the enemy nations, the children would inherit all that belonged to Israel. That could not be allowed to happen because God is faithful to His promises, and God kept His promise to Abraham through using Jacob, who now had the birthright.

Here is what we see in this story about God's grace and mercy being lavished upon those He loves. God spoke to Rebekah while the twins were still in her womb. He made sure Rebekah knew what was happening inside of her when she asked, and He told her what her twin boys represented. God was still in control, and God still kept the promise. Jacob was the one chosen by God Himself, who would go forth, and he would be the father to the twelve tribes of Israel, which would establish

Israel as a nation. Jacob was the one whom God chose for the faithful line of people to come through to bring forth our Messiah Jesus Christ.

As we see throughout the Scriptures, in particular, this story, evil never wins. Esau did not have the heart to seek after God. Esau gave up his birthright, which was spiritual, for a bowl of lentils, which was temporal. That shows us what Esau thought of God. There was nothing righteous about his choices, actions, or attitude. He clearly hated the blessings of God.

What a contrast between righteous living and unrighteous living. Jacob became the father of the twelve tribes of Israel. Esau's descendants were destroyed, as spoken of in the book of Obadiah. Righteous living brings forth blessings. Unrighteous living brings forth destruction and death.

When it comes to living a life of righteousness, it is a matter of the circumcision of the heart. To be circumcised in heart means that you are in a covenant with God, devoted and consecrated to Him, to be used for His glory and His honor. The Abrahamic Covenant had the circumcision of the flesh; however, there was a spiritual aspect of the circumcision of the flesh, and that was the covenant. The circumcision of the flesh was symbolic of the covenant between God and His people. The descendants of Abraham would need to be circumcised in the flesh in order to be part of the covenant between God and His people. Spiritual circumcision is a covenant you make with God to serve Him all the days of your life and obey His ways and His commands. In other words, the spiritual circumcision of the heart means you are now joined in a covenant relationship with God. This means you have set your heart and mind to follow God in all

His ways, radically transformed in the heart from the inside out. This means the hardening of your heart has been broken, the calloused part cut off, creating a new heart that seeks after God, bows down to God alone, and does not yield to another. You have entered a love relationship with God, and nothing can come between you and God and the covenant you have made with Him. Esau did not have the circumcision of the heart. Still, because of the Abrahamic Covenant, we know that he would have had the physical circumcision. However, Esau's outward circumcision didn't matter when his heart was hardened, calloused, and in direct opposition and rebellion toward God. He despised the calling of God on his life, trashed his heritage, acted out in the most despicable behavior, and went after unholy alliances by marrying foreign wives from the enemy nations of Israel, unlike his brother, Jacob. According to his father Isaac's instructions, the latter had gone after only one wife. My point here is that he wanted to marry only Rachel, that was his intention. He was tricked into marrying Leah, so he had two wives. But it's clear in God's word that he loved only Rachel. He was stuck with Leah. The greatest deception amongst those who call themselves ministers or claim to have a relationship with God is that they choose to marry outside of their faith. They decide to marry unbelievers or those who pretend to be believers. Esau was a man who chased after women. He cared only about satisfying and gratifying the lusts of the flesh. Esau had no honor.

Men and women of God, may I humbly remind us that every wicked thing comes from the heart, which clearly means we must circumcise and consecrate our hearts completely to God. Let me give you an example that spells it out: Satan uses social media to get your heart to sin in today's world. It is not far off from what Esau did. He went around marrying anybody. He didn't care where his eyes landed, versus Jacob, who had his eye on one woman named Rachel. Jacob was deceived, but his love was for one woman, Rachel. To live a righteous life, you need to determine in your heart, mind, and spirit not to displease God. You must be vigilant in how you act and how you speak. You must guard your heart.

Study Guide

As we can see in the story of Esau, *"The righteous shall inherit the land, and dwell therein for ever,"* (Psalm 37:29 KJV). We should never be so quick to give up the inheritance that the Lord has given to us. Esau gave up his birthright because he despised it. God has just good things to give His children, good and perfect gifts. Esau was the oldest, and by tradition, he was to receive a double portion of the inheritance his father would bless him with. Instead, he sold out his birthright to his younger brother Jacob. It is foolish to give what is rightfully yours to someone else. When you are handed a godly legacy, you take that godly legacy, and you live it. You run with it. You pass that godly legacy to the next generation. Esau sold his birthright, an eternal birthright, for something temporal - a bowl of lentils. Let us not be like Esau. Let us instead take hold and cling tightly to the God we serve, never giving up our eternal inheritance that we even get to enjoy now, here on the earth, as we are living under the blessings of God.

1. What is the significance of Esau's birthright? Why was it

foolish for Esau to forfeit his inheritance? In forfeiting his birthright, what was Esau losing out on?

2. What was the problem with Esau's choice of wives? Had Esau been blessed by Isaac with the blessing meant for the oldest in the family, what would have happened to their family legacy and inheritance?

3. What happened to the descendants of Esau?

4. Compare circumcision of the heart versus circumcision of the flesh in the Abrahamic Covenant. What are the similarities, and what are the differences?

5. What can we learn about righteous living and unrighteous living from the story of Esau?

CHAPTER 7
PRAISE HIM IN THE WAITING
PART 1

Noah

I enjoy writing about people's lives who made a significant difference in our world. Noah is one of them. I can't believe God could not find anyone, in Noah's days, righteous like him, his wife, his sons, and his daughters-in-law. Do you realize that there were thousands of people living on the earth at that time? The Bible does not tell us how many people lived during Noah's time. There seem to be a few different views on the population. I'm going to offer those views to you, but I will not speculate. I will say that there weren't just a few people that would prompt God to send a flood to destroy everything. The population could have been as high as a few billion. That is something to think about. However, we know by Scriptures that mankind had become incredibly violent and wicked. *"There were giants in the earth in those days; and also after that, when the sons of God came in unto the daughters of men, and they bear children to them, the same became mighty men which were of old, men of renown. And God saw that the wickedness of man was great in the earth, and that every imagination of the thoughts of his heart was only evil continually,"* (Genesis 6:4-5 KJV). By figuring out how long each of Noah's ancestors had lived, Noah would have entered the ark when the earth would have been at least 1,000 years old. Therefore, the population on the earth was definitely not a few hundred or a few thousand people. When we study the Word of God, we always have to remember that there was a world filled with people during the time of the characters we have been studying.

I want to point out that God specifically said what the problem was, who the people who caused it were, and the consequences for their sins. First, God acknowledged that the people were "wicked and evil." This means the people were intent on killing and destroying others. They were wild in every sense of the word. They were rough and aggressive, and if that's not bad enough, they intended to terrorize those around them. They were bloodthirsty and enjoyed their barbaric ways; they were heartless, ruthless, and merciless. They were ferocious bullies, savages, vicious, and brutal. The things they were doing were inhumane. These people were completely out of control. They took no pity on anybody. Did you get the picture? Nobody was safe, and it was only getting worse.

Second, God identified who these vicious and evil people were. When God said they were evil, let me help you understand the kind of evil. These people were diabolical, malicious, and despicable. Their actions were demonic and sinister. They were black-hearted, intent on doing ungodly, unholy, sinful acts.

Everything they did was foul and vile. Do you see the picture clearly here? What strikes me is what God further says, *"that every imagination of the thoughts of his heart was only evil continually."* The word "imagination" is transliterated from the Hebrew word "yetser," which means "conception, framework." Their thoughts did not have in mind the things of God. Because of this, the framework of their thoughts was based solely on man's carnal and selfish ways. Everything they were conceiving in their minds and hearts are the words we used above in the description of wicked and evil. You can understand now that God could no longer look the other way. Notice that God doesn't even bother to tell us the kinds of sins that they were committing; it was that evil, and we can see the punishment God was going to give them: *"And God said unto Noah, The end of all flesh is come before me; for the earth is filled with violence through them; and, behold, I will destroy them with the earth,"* (Genesis 6:13 (KJV). Be careful of what you conceive in your heart. Sin begins in your heart. The mind works off of the heart. What you conceive in your heart will become what you think. What you think will come out in action. Therefore, you repent in your heart and renew your mind by reading the Word of God. This is how you stop going down in a spiral of sin and wickedness.

Third, God told us who these wicked and evil people were. *"There were giants in the earth in those days; and also after that, when the sons of God came in unto the daughters of men, and they bear children to them, the same became mighty men which were of old, men of renown,"* (Genesis 6:4 KJV). The Nephilim, the descendants of Anak, were giants, and they were wreaking havoc on earth. They could no longer be contained. God knew their frame of mind and heart. They weren't going to change, repent, or cooperate with their neighbors or God. Therefore, God took action because not one person other than Noah and his family was found to be righteous. The disaster He was bringing was so horrific and devastating that everything on planet Earth would die and be destroyed at the hands of God.

What's even more astonishing is that no one was found right-eous except for eight people with all the hundreds, thousands, and possibly millions of people. How does that happen? I'll tell you how. Have you ever heard the story of placing a rotten apple in a box of good apples? It is precisely the same principle; this is exactly what happened here. One bad apple placed next to a good apple will contaminate that apple and all the other apples until every apple in the box is infested with worms. One worm produces many, many more worms, contaminating every apple inside the box. Now all the apples have become inedible and rotten, and now must all be thrown out and destroyed. Just like how we don't have an option when our vegetables and fruit become infected and rotten, so it is with the worm of wickedness.

As God's eyes searched among the people of that day, He found a man named Noah, whom the Bible says in Genesis 6:8 (KJV), *"But Noah found grace in the eyes of the Lord."* Due to this grace, Noah was distinguished and handpicked by God to preserve the future generation. When the hand of God rests on a person, the miraculous happens. The unbelievable and the impossible become believable and possible.

Names and their meanings are quite significant throughout this book. I named my son "Noah" because of this Bible verse in

Genesis 6:9 (KJV), *"These are the generations of Noah: Noah was a just man and perfect in his generations, and Noah walked with God."* Take note of how opposite Noah is in his character as opposed to the Nephilim, who were evil. Noah was morally upright and virtuous before God. He was faultless, blameless, and guiltless. He was noble, sensible, and honorable. He was a God-fearing, law-abiding, and high-minded man. He was a man of great worth who was ethical and moral. No wonder God chose him. He had the favor and the glory of God upon his life. Because he lived righteously, he was saved along with his entire family - wife, sons, and daughters-in-law – and, most importantly, he saved his descendants. God kept His creation alive through him. May God find you and me to be like Noah.

What happens next will be difficult to comprehend with our finite minds. In Genesis 6:14-16 (KJV), it says, *"Make thee an ark of gopher wood; rooms shalt thou make in the ark, and shalt pitch it within and without with pitch. And this is the fashion which thou shalt make it of: The length of the ark shall be three hundred cubits, the breadth of it fifty cubits, and the height of it thirty cubits. A window shalt thou make to the ark, and in a cubit shalt thou finish it above; and the door of the ark shalt thou set in the side thereof; with lower, second, and third stories shalt thou make it."* Let me break down these cubit measurements into feet. Noah's ark was approximately 450 feet long, 75 feet wide, and 45 feet high, conservatively speaking. This ark would have been over one and a half football fields in length, including the end zones. It would have been approximately taller than a four-story house. This was no small task.

Let's talk about the gopher wood. This word is mentioned only once in the Bible, as the material used by Noah to build the ark.

The Hebrew word "gofer" is transliterated into English as "gopher," which means "cypress." This tree is tall. It is an ever-green tree, and it stands upright. It is also described as having great durability. No wonder the ancient world took much value in this type of wood for shipbuilding. Before I explain any further, I want to pause and take a good look at the description of this tree: a tall, upright evergreen tree with great durability.

The Scriptures tell us in Isaiah 61:3 (KJV), *"To appoint unto them that mourn in Zion, to give unto them beauty for ashes, the oil of joy for mourning, the garment of praise for the spirit of heaviness; that they might be called trees of righteousness, the planting of the LORD, that he might be glorified."* (Please refer to Psalm 1:3, 92:12; Proverbs 11:28, Job 29:19 for further reference on being like trees of righteousness.) Do you see the comparison described of the cypress tree and the kind of tree we should be? Before God, we are to walk uprightly with a pure heart. This means we are obeying Him and living according to His laws. By doing what God has commanded and living as He wants us to live, we live uprightly and walk in righteousness. We are like trees planted by the water that produce the fruits of holiness and right-eousness. Even the type of tree God chose to build the ark was described as a "righteous" tree. God uses everything.

Like the gopher wood, each tree has been designed with a purpose. Each has its work to produce. Noah used the gopher wood because first, God instructed him to use the gopher wood, and second, the gopher wood was the perfect substance to use to make the quality of boat that God had in store for Noah to make. Let's compare the gopher wood to the fig tree that Jesus cursed. Jesus was off in the distance, He saw the fig tree and the leaves on the fig tree, so he went over to the tree. Jesus got there and saw the blossoms, but He saw no fruit. The fig tree showed blossoms, promising there would be fruit, but Jesus found that the tree had no fruit. Therefore, because the fig tree did not produce the figs it was supposed to, Jesus cursed the tree; the tree withered up and died the moment He spoke.

Creation is responsible to its Maker, and that, my friends, includes you and me. Let's dig a little bit deeper. Spiritually speaking, you see, the cypress trees were able to be used to protect and sustain the lives of Noah, his wife, his sons, and their wives. They protected the future of mankind; in addition, they protected every single species known to man, both male and female: animals, insects, fowl, etc. In contrast, there once was a fig tree. That fig tree was standing in the right location at the right time. It was the beginning of the season for figs to grow. Now, let me share with you that figs are my favorite fruit. I grew up in Italy, and we had fig trees. Therefore, I can tell you that some of our fig trees would produce what we called the first fruit. We could see the buds of the actual little figs in April, and the bigger ones would come out in May. Then the little ones that we could also see would be ready sometime in August. We would often still have figs up until October. The fig trees were deceiving because you could see them as if they were alive by their beautiful green leaves. Still, when you went to look on the branches, you would know immediately if the tree was rotten or not, or if the tree could even be saved. My grandfather, Paolo, would know immediately if the tree could be saved by pruning it to see whether or not it would produce figs the following year. If not, the fig tree would be cut right then and there. This is what Jesus did. He knew the tree could not be saved. Can you see the importance of this analogy that we paused for? In the Bible, God describes us as a tree planted by the water. The water is life to the tree. Jesus Christ is living water that we drink from to sustain our spiritual life. Without Him, we can do nothing.

There are only two options, only two. You can either flourish like the tree planted by the water, producing the fruits of righteousness, or be like the fig tree and cut off. If you are going to be like a tree planted by the water, then you will care about living a holy and righteous life before God, bringing others to Christ and helping them in their walk with the Lord, and obeying the laws of God. Your main goal will be to seek God's approval in all you do and say. However, suppose you are the fig tree, just pretending and only playing the part. In that case, eventually, God will have to cut you off because He knows there is nothing good in you that will produce any fruit; not even pruning you will benefit you in your future relationship with God or help anyone around you.

Now, look at this generation of Noah and his family and the times they were living in. Please understand this. They were in the world, but not of the world. Their lives were lived in righteousness. Therefore, Noah found favor in the eyes of God as we saw earlier. *"But Noah found grace in the eyes of the Lord,"* (Genesis 6:8 KJV). In other words, Noah was upright before God, able to receive from the Lord. God was able to use his righteous life because he did not bow down to the evil and wicked things happening in his generation. Like Noah, we are to live a holy and acceptable life before the holy and righteous God. I would like to note that we often hear people say that it took about one hundred years to build the ark, but we can find nowhere in Scripture where it gives a time for how long it took to build the ark. I believe that is because God was in control. This was a monumental task with no modern-day equipment or technology. It would have taken the Spirit of God to do whatever needed to be done to complete that which God spoke to Noah. Imagine cutting down trees for this project and collecting all the other material needed to build this ark and hold it together. However, I would like to point out a couple of things. After Noah finished building the ark, imagine the patience of God as He waited to see if anyone from Noah's generation would have a change of heart and repent from their wicked ways. Since that didn't happen, God began to prepare the animals to come into the ark. We always hear how they went in two by two, but that's not what happened. Let me explain to you what happened, according to the Word of God, found in Genesis 7:1-4 (KJV), *"And the Lord said unto Noah, Come thou and all thy house into the ark; for thee have I seen righteous before me in this generation. Of every clean beast thou shalt take to thee by sevens, the male and his female: and of beasts that are not clean by two, the male and his female. Of fowls also of the air by sevens, the male and the female; to keep seed alive upon the face of all the earth. For yet seven days, and I will cause it to rain upon the earth forty days and forty nights; and every living substance that I have made will I destroy from off the face of the earth."* Did you catch that? There weren't just two of each unclean animal, male and female, boarding the ark. There were seven of each of the clean animals, male and female, boarding the ark. I believe God gives us a picture here. God longs to shower His people with blessings and goodness. He was tripling that which was good for man back on the earth. At the same time, you see His goodness and His mercy by not destroying the unclean animals after Adam and Eve's fall. Personally, I wish He would have allowed every snake on the face of the earth to disappear. If this does not show the mercy and love of God even in the lives of animals He created, I don't know what does. The second thing that happened here is God gave him only seven days. It took six days for God to create the earth, and He rested on the seventh, and now God was going to destroy everything on the seventh day, the day He rested. Please take note, God had every animal lining up to go into that ark. The animals not only went up to the ark, but they also knew where to go. They weren't being waved in or checked. They boarded the ark and went to their compartments. There was no such thing as animals trying to eat each other or striking out at each other. They simply did as God commanded them. There are some things the human mind cannot comprehend or fathom. This is one of them, when we do not think with the spiritual mind. Let's also take note of God's command to Noah, *"Come thou and all thy house into the ark...."* This is what it is like for us as children of God. God is like the ark. When you are doing things God's way, following His commands, and doing His will, you are in the ark of safety even if the storms of life are hitting, whether the times are good or bad. You are safe. Literally, God was saying to Noah, "Come here into the boat. I am with you, and I will not allow anything to happen to you. I am protecting you, your family, and every creature on the face of the Earth." What a beautiful representation of God's invitation to His mercy, grace, and love. Just like God was with Noah in the ark, so was Jesus in the boat with His disciples when the storm struck the lake. Just as Jesus kept the disciples safe, God kept Noah safe. Presently, the Holy Spirit who resides in us and is God's presence within us keeps us safe. He is the very breath of Christ.

Finally, it was the hand of God who shut the door of the ark, and we see this in Genesis 7:16 (KJV): *"and the LORD shut him in."* The Lord shut him in, and the Lord also told him when to open the door, which we can see in Genesis 8:15-16 (KJV). *"And God spake unto Noah, saying, Go forth of the ark, thou, and thy wife, and thy sons, and thy sons' wives with thee."* God shutting the door has great significance in more than just one way. I want to point out that God's instruction to Noah is where to put the door. In Genesis 6:16, God told Noah to set the door on the side of the ark. Notice how there is one door to get in and out of the ark. We know of another door spoken of in John 10:9 (KJV). *"I am the door: by me if any man enter in, he shall be saved, and shall go in and out, and find pasture."* Do you understand the great significance of this? God had said to Noah to come into the ark, which we already discussed that He, God Himself, was in the ark with Noah. Noah and his family entered through the only door on the ark to be saved from the wrath, judgment, and destruction unleashed on the wicked. Now Jesus says He is the door and invites you to come in. That is an invitation. The invitation is still being given today to enter through the only door which will keep you safe and away from the destruction that befalls the unrighteous. Jesus made it very clear when He said He is the only Way to come to the Father; there is no other way. Second, it took faith for Noah and his family to be locked in with only one way of escape, one door, which God Himself had shut.

Let's be real. There were venomous snakes, tigers, lions, bears, crocodiles, and many other vicious and deadly animals, not just cute and friendly animals. They literally had to trust God to keep them safe, even from the animals in the ark. So, it is the same with us. We are saved by grace through faith, not by anything we have done.

Finally, when God shuts the door, no one can open that door; nothing will be able to open that door. God opens the door for salvation, but we have to walk through the door just like Noah at the end of God's judgment and wrath upon the earth. Then, when it was time for Noah to leave the ark, God instructed him to go forth with his family and all the animals, which meant Noah was able to now open the door, and he did.

I want you to clearly understand something important from these verses. Notice how God Himself shut the door behind Noah and his family. It was not Noah who shut the door. It was God who shut the door. Is it possible that God shut the door because Noah, who was righteous, would have let people in when the floodwaters started to rise and people began drowning? Friends, relatives, neighbors...People he spoke with every day and ran to? These are the people God found unrighteous. Remember, it was only Noah and his immediate family that was saved. Can you imagine being aboard the ark and hearing the screams of men, women, and children as they were drowning? They had the chance to board the ark and be saved from sin's disastrous consequences, yet they chose not to. *"Therefore shall evil come upon thee; thou shalt not know from whence it riseth: and mischief shall fall upon thee; thou shalt not be able to put it off: and desolation shall come upon thee suddenly, which thou shalt not know,"* (Isaiah 47:11 KJV), and *"They did eat, they drank, they married wives, they were given in marriage, until the day that Noah entered into the ark, and the flood came, and destroyed them all,"* (Luke 17:27 KJV).

It is heartbreaking to me when I know that no matter what I say and how much I pray, there will be those around me who will reject God. These Bible verses are very clear. Unfortunately, there will be people in our lives who will die who have not accepted Jesus Christ into their lives. This has nothing to do with you and me. This has to do with their decisions and choices to reject Jesus Christ as Lord and Savior of their lives. It's painful to read this statement, but nonetheless, it is the Spirit of the living God who draws all men unto Him. The Holy Spirit convicts us of our sins and points to the Lord Jesus Christ, the Savior and Lord of our lives. It is not you and I who can save anybody. Sometimes God will shut a door on a relationship or on a person because God knows the heart. This is why God closed the door Himself after Noah and his family boarded the ark. All of the giants put together, at that time, would not have been able to penetrate that door. Please listen carefully. *"These things saith he that is holy, he that is true, he that hath the key of David, he that openeth, and no man shutteth; and shutteth, and no man openeth,"* (Revelation 3:7 KJV).

"...by me if any man enter in, he shall be saved, and shall go in and out, and find pasture," (John 10:9 KJV). Jesus Christ is the door by which we go in and out. Let me explain. Jesus gives us liberty. In other words, you have freedom. You can walk without guilt, shame, and condemnation. His Spirit lives in you, and where His Spirit is, there is freedom. While we have boundaries, those boundaries are not meant to destroy our fun; they are intended to protect us. We get to live in pleasant and green pastures. Our minds and our souls are at rest. He is our yokebearer, meaning He will carry all our problems and anxieties, no matter what

storms come our way. You are protected just as Noah was in the ark. Jesus is your ark of safety.

What happens next upon opening the door and Noah and his family stepping out is very significant and should speak volumes to us. Look at what Noah does in Genesis 8:20-21 (KJV). *"And Noah builded an altar unto the Lord; and took of every clean beast, and of every clean fowl, and offered burnt offerings on the altar. And the Lord smelled a sweet savour; and the Lord said in his heart, I will not again curse the ground any more for man's sake; for the imagination of man's heart is evil from his youth; neither will I again smite any more every thing living, as I have done."* Notice Noah's behavior and attitude. He went off the ark with his family and all the animals, and his first righteous act before doing anything else was to offer sacrifices of thanksgiving to God for His protection and salvation from the floodwaters that wiped out every living thing off the face of the earth. Up to this point, God had instructed Noah on how to build the ark, what wood to use, the animals that would go on it, who could go on the boat (him and his family), when to get on it, and when to get out of the ark, even telling Noah what He was going to do to all the people and animals on the earth. When it was time for him to leave the ark, the only thing God told him was that he could get off the ark. There's never any instruction from God about making a sacrifice. Noah did that out of a heart of gratitude, appreciation, thankfulness, and devotion to God. This act of Noah's was acknowledging what God had done. It was the most respectful and honoring act, giving glory to God for what God had just done.

Let me remind you, Noah's daughters-in-law had family— parents, sisters, brothers, aunts, uncles, nephews, nieces, cousins, and perhaps grandparents. Noah's family would have had friends, too. Imagine the ridicule they had to suffer because God gave a command to Noah to build an ark. May I remind us that there was no ocean near them? You do not build an ark of such magnitude with no water in sight, and how would you get it to water when you have nothing to haul a ship of that size? In addition, the earth had not seen rain up to this point. We know that when God created Adam and Eve, there was no rain coming from the sky. What happened after the exile from the garden? The earth was no longer perfect. I personally believe that there was no rain as we experience rain today. My reason is because I have done a complete study of the four major studies of geology, meteorology, astronomy, and oceanography of Earth Sciences. Those researchers and experts who I have learned from, in their respective fields, were both Christian and non-Christian and some atheists. They could prove the possibility that the earth did not experience the type of rain seen during the flood.

Let me give you a little science lesson. We get rainbows after it rains. We all know that rainbows are created by the refraction of light passing through suspended water, or as we call it, "water drops." There is no mention of rainbows until after the flood when God put the rainbow in the sky, found in Genesis 9:12-13 (KJV). *"And God said, This is the token of the covenant which I make between me and you and every living creature that is with you, for perpetual generations: I do set my bow in the cloud, and it shall be for a token of a covenant between me and the earth."* Do I believe that there was absolutely no water for the earth to replenish? Am I suggesting that there was absolutely no water on earth to replenish the water supply for drinking water or to produce vegetation? Obviously not. We all know that water is a major life-supporting resource. I'm simply explaining that those people did not ever experience rain, that type of a heavy rain. Whatever rain they experienced, and however God did it, it definitely was not in the capacity you and I understand rain today.

It is not hard to believe that, before the flood, there could have been very little to no rain at all. Genesis 7:11, 24 and 8:4 seem to indicate that five months consisted of one hundred and fifty days. This makes sense that the days before the flood were a little longer than what we experience today as a twenty-four-hour day. The earth was a lush tropical forest with abundant vegetation, even without rain in Noah's day. Because the days were longer, that meant more sunlight and warmer temperatures. After this catastrophic flood, the earth's ecosystem changed. Please understand, before God allowed the rain to fall, there would not have been atmospheric turbulences, and there would have been less wind. We know that winds are caused by the temperature differential resulting from the tilt of the Earth's axis, ice caps, and mountain systems. These things cause unequal regions of hot and cold around the globe. Before the flood, the Earth was actually warmer, and we also had smaller oceans. Our atmosphere, before the flood, did not have the conditions for rain to condense compared to what we see today. The particles that we call "condensation nuclei" are vital in forming water droplets. If this is the case, it signifies the Earth, before the flood, had much smaller oceans and, obviously, no rain. The particles for water drops and their production would have been minuscule and/or nonexistent. They wouldn't have been able to form. In addition, the Earth would have experienced less atmospheric turbulence.

Then came the flood. The waters had to recede. When this occurred, it changed everything, meaning weather patterns, storms, and the hours in a day. It is important to note that even if there was little or no rain before the flood, it does not in any way, form, or shape indicate that the Earth was not one huge dry place. Understanding what I just explained, the Earth would have been a much warmer place and heavy with moisture that was not condensed, which implies there would have been an extremely capable, useful, and effective condensation cycle. From this perspective, condensed water droplets would have been larger and more normal, meaning this took place daily. The Earth's surface, at night, would have cooled very quickly, which would make the planet competent enough to create its own heavy mist or fog. Then it would sense that the Earth was watered this way each day. This is the position I personally take after studying what the experts of various earth sciences say, and the science clearly shows the Bible to be valid.

I just explained my personal position of no rain before the flood. Whatever position we take is not the point. The point is that destruction fell because of the wicked, evil, and unrighteous behavior of Noah's day.

God did find righteousness on Earth. He found it within Noah and his family. God could not find anyone outside of Noah's family who was righteous. He found not one other living soul like Noah and his family. The people of that time were found by God to be wicked and evil as shown in Genesis 8: 21 (KJV),: "...*for the imagination of man's heart is evil from his youth...*" Noah had a position in his family. Noah was the spiritual leader to his family, the covering for his wife, and the protector of his wife and sons and his daughters-in-law. He had a mandate from God with specific instructions to save himself and his entire household. Noah simply obeyed God, and he followed every instruction given to him, and in the order God gave. Noah took his standing before God very seriously, and God lavished him with grace. Righteousness produces this kind of life.

Study Guide

As we can see in the story of Noah, *"Noah was a just man and perfect in his generations, and Noah walked with God,"* (Genesis 6:9 KJV). Noah and his family were found to be righteous. However, the world was about to come under God's judgment, and God had provided a way to save Noah and his family. It is essential to be in the ark of God's safety. We learn this in the story of Noah. Mankind was so out of control that God was going to wipe them out. They brought on themselves destruction and death. Let's take a lesson from the story of Noah. It is better to live righteously and be a friend of God than to live an unrighteous life and be God's enemy.

1. What was mankind like in the days of Noah? Can you compare the time of Noah with the times we are living in? Explain.

2. What was God going to bring to the Earth as a result of man's ways? Keeping in mind that Noah and his family were righteous, what was God going to do for Noah and his family?

3. Why did Noah offer sacrifices to God when they had come off the ark? Even though God never instructed Noah to do it, why was this so important?

4. Compare Noah's ark to Jesus. What are the similarities between Noah's ark and Jesus?

5. What kind of life does righteousness produce? Explain.

CHAPTER 8
PRAISE HIM IN THE WAITING
PART 2

Judas

Judas Iscariot's name has become synonymous with those who betray us today. This is a name of disgrace, shame, dishonor, and offense. I don't know about you, but I have yet to meet someone named "Judas." Names mean something. We associate character with someone's name. I was floored when I learned the biblical meaning of the name "Judas." The name "Judas" means "praise" or "the praised one." His parents, upon his birth, gave him one of the greatest names with a beautiful meaning. Their son, Judas, was to be praised for his contributions to his generation in our world. There was a destiny to be fulfilled, and it was noteworthy. He was to bring praise. Judas could have been known as a godly example of a life lived out to serve Christ, but that didn't happen. Instead of being celebrated and people praising him, he is remembered as the one who betrayed the Savior of all mankind, Jesus Christ. His name is a name that makes us cringe and provokes feelings of disgust and anger. How could he have done this to our Lord and Savior, Jesus Christ?

Imagine this with me, and please take note of the spiritual connotation. Look at what Jesus did before choosing the disciples. In Luke 6:12-16 (KJV), it says, *"And it came to pass in those days, that he went out into a mountain to pray, and continued all night in prayer to God. And when it was day, he called unto him his disciples: and of them he chose twelve, whom also he named apostles; Simon, (whom he also named Peter,) and Andrew his brother, James and John, Philip and Bartholomew, Matthew and Thomas, James the son of Alphaeus, and Simon called Zelotes, And Judas the brother of James, and Judas Iscariot, which also was the traitor."* There are several things that occurred in this passage. The first thing that Jesus did was to go up into the mountain and pray. Like all the Bible prophets had done, Jesus went into a secluded place to spend time with His Heavenly Father. In this passage, Jesus went up the mountain to pray so His communion with God would not be interrupted. The prophets of old went to the mountains to be alone with God. When God called Moses, Moses had to go to the mountain; that's where Moses saw the glory of God. It was on the mountain where the ten commandments were given, not once, but twice. When Moses came down from the mountain, the glory of God was upon him and had shone so brightly that a veil had to be put over him. Abraham had to go to the mountain to make the sacrifice, and it was there where he saw the provision of God. Elisha went to the mountain, and it was in that quiet place of seclusion where Elisha heard God speak in the still small voice; there, he heard clearly. Elisha was on the mountain when the fire fell from Heaven upon the altar and consumed the sacrifice and the water in the mote around the altar, revealing who the true God really is. Caleb went to the mountain, and it was on that mountain that he saw God defeat his enemies and make him victorious.

Here we see Jesus Christ, the Son of God, go to the mountain. Here, God launched Him to the purpose and plans that He had for Him and mankind. This is where He and God discussed who the disciples would be, including the last disciple, Judas Iscariot, who was immediately known to be the one to betray Jesus. Going to the mountain is very important in each believer's life because it is where you and God meet alone. Here is where your destiny and the purposes and plans God has for your life will be revealed.

Second, He prayed. There are plenty of examples of those men mentioned above who prayed. Let me just give you a few. In the wilderness, Moses was constantly praying for the Israelites who often disobeyed God. Abraham had prayed for God to provide the animal to be sacrificed upon the mountain when he was with Isaac. Elisha prayed that God would reveal Himself from Heaven by sending fire down to consume the sacrifice and water on the altar. Caleb prayed for his inheritance. Jesus was now praying for who would be His disciples.

No great destiny was ever fulfilled without prayer.

Third, He continued on in prayer and He prayed through the night. One cannot pray without perseverance and determination. Jesus persevered the entire night in prayer. He didn't give up. Neither did Moses, Abraham, Elisha, or Caleb. For their destinies to come about, and for God's purposes and plans for them to be fulfilled, they had to be in communion with God. That meant each had to get alone with God to hear from Him.

Moses spent time in prayer on the mountain, talking with God, and getting instructions from God. In prayer, Abraham was promised a son and that his descendants would be many. Elisha sought refuge and comfort in prayer as he was being chased down by Jezebel, and it was in prayer that he heard the voice of God. Caleb knew God's promise for Israel and knew what his inheritance would be because he spent time in prayer, communing with God.

The fourth thing Jesus did was to go and take action. Please pay attention to this very carefully. What you hear on the mountaintop must be put into action or you will forfeit the promises of God. This is where most people fail. They do not adhere to the specific instructions that God gives them. Imagine for a moment if Moses didn't persevere. He wouldn't have seen or experienced the glory of God. Imagine if Abraham had not gone to sacrifice Isaac. He wouldn't have seen God's provision of the ram, nor would he have heard the heart of God regarding his future. Elisha would not have heard the still small voice and learned the truth that he was not the only one who didn't bow down to Baal. He could take courage because God was protecting him. Caleb wouldn't have conquered the biggest mountain and received the biggest blessing to shower on all his children. Jesus was already prepared for the betrayal that was to come from one of His own disciples.

Please listen. It is at the mountaintop where God gives us His instructions. Don't bother going to seek God's counsel in prayer if you are not going to follow through on the instructions He already gave you. It's up to us to persevere and follow the instructions completely as He has told them to us. Either we receive the promises because we persevered and didn't give up, or we completely forfeit and lose the promises of God.

I find it amazing how many chances God will give a person to make things right with Him. We have all been betrayed by a Judas in our midst. Judas was with Jesus daily. He heard the teachings, and he followed Jesus everywhere. Judas would have witnessed the blind receiving their sight, the lame being able to walk, the deaf being able to hear, fevers leaving, the demon-possessed being set free, and people coming to life. Yet after seeing all of this, his heart was still hardened. Catch this: you can have the best mentor or teacher, but your mentors cannot do anything for you unless you have the heart to grow. In this case with Judas, he was with Jesus Christ, the Messiah, and was in His presence daily, and still, Judas' heart was as cold as ice. He was like a rock surrounded by water, but Christ couldn't penetrate his heart because Judas was evil and wicked to the core of his being. Please listen. You can know about Jesus, and He can heal you, give you the desires of your heart, and show you miracle after miracle, but you can still betray Him. If you have your heart and mind made up not to follow Christ, it won't matter what Christ does for you.

Claiming to be a Christian is not what saves you, nor does it mean you are in a relationship with Christ. Following a religion doesn't save you. The only thing that saves us is Jesus Christ. This means accepting Jesus as your personal Savior into your heart and life. You literally have a change of heart, turning from your old life outside of Christ, and now inside of Christ, you are a new creation. The old you is gone. Now you are new, just like a newborn baby. Judas never accepted Christ.

We see a trend in Judas' behavior and character. Let's look at this passage found in John 12:2-6 (KJV). *"There they made him a supper; and Martha served: but Lazarus was one of them that sat at the table with him. Then took Mary a pound of ointment of spikenard, very costly, and anointed the feet of Jesus, and wiped his feet with her hair: and the house was filled with the odour of the ointment. Then saith one of his disciples, Judas Iscariot, Simon's son, which should betray him, Why was not this ointment sold for three hundred pence, and given to the poor? This he said, not that he cared for the poor; but because he was a thief, and had the bag, and bare what was put therein."* Judas was selfishly motivated. He didn't care about the poor. Judas cared about the money. Let me pause here and explain something clearly. Everything Jesus did was for the poor and the hurting. He fed the multitudes. He had compassion for the widows who were treated horribly in those days. He had compassion for the sick little girl and showed how much compassion He had. He raised the widow's son back to life. He even had compassion with the woman who had the issue of blood, who should never have touched Him. How about the woman at the well and the woman caught in the act of adultery? How about going and casting the demons out of the man who was terrorizing the town despite the people who chased Him away? How about at his last moment on the cross when He forgave the criminal on the cross next to Him? Jesus was all about compassion, love, forgiveness, restoration, and healing. You can understand why this comment from a ruthless, evil man would be poor in judgment and appalling. Judas' heart was speaking at that moment. I've learned the hard way to pay attention to what people say. We tend to look at the action and not really hear what people are saying. Truth is revealed both in speech and in action together.

I started this chapter by giving the biblical meaning of the name "Judas." We have said that his parents looked upon their newborn child and thought so highly of him that they named him "praise." Every time those parents called his name, praise is what he heard. What he should have done was to bring honor not only to God but also to his family. Instead, we see his real character and the ugliness of his heart. There was nothing righteous about Judas. There was nothing to praise him about.

The real issue here has nothing to do with the meaning of his name, because he didn't live up to the meaning of his name. It is really about a person's character, integrity, honor, self-respect, and moral fortitude. It is all about character. Judas' character is best described as destructive. He lived a disastrous life. What he did was disgraceful to his name and to his family. He grieved his biological family, and, at this point, his spiritual family, which were the other eleven disciples. More importantly, he grieved the Spirit of the Living God. He brought horrifying consequences upon Jesus, who was convicted as a criminal. Do you see the full picture of what was done to Jesus? His entire life was miserable. His life was regrettable, as we know from this passage in Matthew 26:24 (KJV). *"The Son of man goeth as it is written of him: but woe unto that man by whom the Son of man is betrayed! it had been good for that man if he had not been born."* Judas was truly a wretched man. He was a reprehensible individual. His life became tragic. Instead of bringing praise, he brought dishonor. His life was like the *Titanic*. It was pitiful and sickening to the core. I'm not sure of anyone else, other than Ahab and Jezebel, that had a worse ending.

At the time of the Last Supper, Jesus knew His time was near, that He would soon be handed over to be crucified. Let's look at the passage found in Matthew 26:24-25 (KJV). *"The Son of man goeth as it is written of him: but woe unto that man by whom the Son of man is betrayed! it had been good for that man if he had not been born. Then Judas, which betrayed him, answered and said, Master, is it I? He said unto him, Thou hast said."* To me, this is a very powerful verse for so many reasons. Let's break it down. Jesus made such a statement regarding the person who would betray Him. He said what would happen to the person who betrayed Him. What part of "woe" did Judas not get? The word "ouai" is transliterated to the English word "woe," which means "exclamation of grief." It is beyond comprehension how Judas heard Jesus say, "...but woe unto that man by whom the Son of man is betrayed..." and continued with his plan to betray. As a parent, when my angelic children push the limit, I start off by holding my hand straight out and saying, "Whoa!" My kids know that when I say "Whoa," they should stop immediately what they are saying or doing. This is what Jesus was saying. Even up until the last moment, he was trying to get Judas' attention with all the love and mercy of God. How much more loathsome could Judas be to still pretend to be a friend of Jesus and pretend to be a disciple after this exchange of words? Jesus was on the mountaintop praying for an entire night. He knew what His mandate on earth was. He already knew the heart of Judas, and yet, He gave Judas an opportunity to repent. God's love knows no bounds. The audacity of Judas is astonishing. His pride and arrogance were beyond comprehension.

Watch Judas' response, *"Is it I, Lord?"* Out of all the malicious, disgusting, and horrible questions to ask, knowing that he would follow through anyway with the betrayal, he asks Jesus if it's him. Jesus was not going to allow Judas to mock Him. Jesus doesn't miss a beat. What Jesus said in response basically was, "You know it's you. Why are you asking?" Again, it's like with our children when we give them a warning and they pretend that they did nothing wrong.

Finally, the scariest thing happens. Let's look at John 13:26-27 (KJV). *"Jesus answered, He it is, to whom I shall give a sop, when I have dipped it. And when he had dipped the sop, he gave it to Judas Iscariot, the son of Simon. And after the sop Satan entered into him. Then said Jesus unto him, That thou doest, do quickly."* Jesus dipped the bread in the wine and offered it to Judas, and Judas took it, missing Christ's second warning. Let's pause for just a moment. We are never to take communion in an unworthy manner like Judas because of this reason. When you partake of communion, you observe the Lord's sacrifice made at Calvary. His suffering is not something to be mocked or scoffed. When Judas took the bread that Christ offered and ate it, He mocked Christ, and then *"Satan entered into him."* Now Satan took over Judas and possessed him. You know that saying, "what possessed you?" In this case, Satan possessed Judas because Judas never belonged to Christ. Judas never had a heart for Christ, and because he wasn't filled with the things of God, Satan took over. What a sad ending. It is heart-wrenching to be separated from Christ for all eternity. If you think this still doesn't happen today, think again.

We can only serve one of two masters. We either serve Jesus or we serve Satan. The highway is filled with people on the fast track to Hell. As sad as my next statement will be, the truth still remains. Every individual on planet Earth must decide on their own to surrender their life to Jesus Christ and live for eternity. Jesus Himself could not change the heart of Judas, even up until the final moment and the two warnings. Do you ever wonder why Jesus warned him three times? There was the warning when he complained about the ointment being spilled out and then the two warnings at the last supper. Now Jesus told him to go do what he was going to do and do it quickly. May we never hear these words spoken to us by Jesus. Of course, Judas got up and went to do his evil deed quickly. At this point, there was no more reasoning with him. Satan had completely overtaken his heart, mind, and soul.

When Satan enters a person, the results are catastrophic, as we can see in the case of Judas. Notice how Satan and sin are interwoven together. Judas was overtaken by Satan, and he went to see the chief priests. Let's look at Matthew 26:14-16 (KJV), *"Then one of the twelve, called Judas Iscariot, went unto the chief priests, And said unto them, What will ye give me, and I will deliver him unto you? And they covenanted with him for thirty pieces of silver. And from that time he sought opportunity to betray him."* Notice that the chief priests made a contract with Judas that Judas would deliver Jesus into their hands. This was all motivated by the love of money. Is it any wonder why the Scriptures say that the love of money is the root of all evil? Judas betrayed Jesus for thirty pieces of silver.

The thirty shekels of silver disturbs me a great deal. Let me explain. There is a mention of thirty pieces of silver in Zechariah 11. The thirty pieces of silver were used to determine the value of a slave according to Jewish law in Exodus 21. When the prophet Zechariah asked the Israelites to pay him his wages because he had done work for them, the Israelites gave him thirty pieces of silver. Those thirty pieces of silver were an insult to God and Zechariah. Therefore, God told Zechariah to throw it back in their faces. You can see Matthew using the same language. It was an insult to Jesus. They treated Jesus as a slave. I can't fathom how Judas could betray someone who treated him so kindly with such a great evil by accepting a contract for a very cheap amount of money. You can see clearly here that sin blinds you and makes you act foolishly without any common sense. Sin may seem gratifying in the momentary pleasure it gives you while doing it. Still, in the end, there is remorse and absolutely no satisfaction.

Just a few hours before, Judas had the last supper with Jesus and the rest of the disciples. I guess when Jesus said to him to do quickly what he must do, Judas didn't waste any time. Isn't this how sin is? Once you open the door to the lusts of the flesh, there is no going back. Once you have determined in your heart and mind to commit the act, there is no stopping you. There is no time to think things through. You quickly run right into a trap, and the trap that Satan leads you into is never pleasant and never ends well. There is great significance in Judas kissing Jesus. That wasn't just a "Hey, how are you doing" kind of kiss. It had great meaning. In those days, it was a sign of respect and honor. Judas was showing no honor or respect to Jesus. This is the reason why Jesus said to him, *"Judas, betrayest thou the Son of man with a kiss?"* In other words, "I just spoke to you a few hours ago. I gave you opportunities to change your mind and repent. You actually took the piece of bread from my hands that I gave to you first. I honored you by giving it to you first, and this is how you are going to repay me, by giving me a disrespectful kiss." You see, sin makes you completely imbecilic. You lose every ounce of sense, self-respect, and integrity because your choice to sin has proven you to be a fool. This is what Jesus was saying to Judas. Here is another point for us to seriously consider. Up to this point, the other eleven disciples did not know that Judas was the traitor. Now they knew who the betrayer of the twelve was, the man they called brother, friend, and confidant. The very man chosen to work in the kingdom had now done the unimaginable, betraying Jesus and all of them. That man was standing face to face with them. The apostles reacted and asked Jesus, "Shall we pick up the sword and fight?" Who do you think would have been killed first that night if Jesus had said yes? Some people do evil and mean-spirited things to us, and our impulse is to want to strike back. However, Jesus knew what was coming, and because of God's divine will and plan, Jesus knew that this all had to be played out. Judas had already sunk himself. In Matthew 27:3-4 (KJV), it says, *"Then Judas, which had betrayed him, when he saw that he was condemned, repented himself, and brought again the thirty pieces of silver to the chief priests and elders, Saying, I have sinned in that I have betrayed the innocent blood. And they said, What is that to us? see thou to that."* If you think that Judas truly repented, no, he did not. The Bible clearly states that, in fact, Jesus Himself had said of Judas, *"The Son of Man will go just as it is written about him, but woe to that man who betrays the Son of Man! It would be better for him if he had not been born."* If Judas was truly sorry for what he had done, he would have gone straight to Jesus to make things right with Him. Judas already had a contract, a covenant, and a signature with those evil high priests. They were never going to undo what they had been plotting for weeks. The sad truth is, directly and immediately after the sin and lust is fulfilled, you hate what you have done and repent. You become like Judas, remorseful. You want to make things right. You want the slate clean. You want to find peace and tranquility. You want the ugly scene to be forgotten. Friends, for those who are truly repentant, God forgives. However, it doesn't work this way for everybody. It didn't work that way with Judas, and it won't work that way for you and me if we are not truly repentant. God already knew the heart of Judas. He knew Judas was not truly repentant for what he had done. God knew that Judas was only sorry for being caught in the act. Now everyone knew the sin that Judas committed. Let us remember that Jesus forgave everyone who asked for forgiveness. Even as we mentioned before, He forgave the criminal on the cross. Surely, He would have done the same if Judas had truly repented as the criminal on the cross did. The saddest story in the Bible for me is the life of Judas. There is absolutely no excuse that could justify what Judas did.

Finally, we see the ending to this twelfth disciple called Judas Iscariot found in Matthew 27:5 (KJV), *"And he cast down the pieces of silver in the temple, and departed, and went and hanged himself."* Zechariah 11 all over again. The high priest had bought Jesus for thirty pieces of silver as if Jesus was a nobody and worthless. Jesus did so many miracles and wonders during His three-year ministry that John 21:25 (KJV) says, *"And there are also many other things which Jesus did, the which, if they should be written every one, I suppose that even the world itself could not contain the books that should be written. Amen."* And the high priest set his value at a measly thirty pieces of silver to show disregard, disrespect, and disdain toward all that Jesus did. Matthew's account is that this was just as disrespectful an act as what happened to Zechariah when God told him to throw back the silver in the Israelites' faces for devaluing the work Zechariah had done. Now we see Judas Iscariot taking the thirty pieces of silver and throwing it in the faces of the high priest and his council. Jesus Christ, the Son of God, was not a slave, but He was the Savior and Redeemer. He came to release us from the power of death and the grave and the law of sin and death. Jesus got treated as a slave by Judas being paid thirty pieces of silver, and God wasn't going to have it. As evil as Judas was, God had the final justice. Be very careful what you do.

The saddest thing for me is to watch people self-destruct. I have watched countless people refuse to change, repent, and humble themselves. I chose to write about Judas because I want us to understand that there is nothing you or I can do to change a person's heart. The Bible states that only God knows the depth of a person's heart. We can model godly behavior. We can walk the walk. We can beg, plead, and wrestle. We can give chance after chance after chance, and still, the person will do what he or she set his or her heart and mind to do. Jesus could not change the heart and mind of Judas. Because Judas was not willing to change and would have continued on his destructive path, Jesus was the one who said, "Go do what you are going to do quickly." The position we take as Christians is that we pray for the lost. We don't give up on anyone, but at the same time, we must understand that, ultimately, decisions are made by the individual. Unfortunately, as we have seen in this book, some sins have been committed, which caused eternal separation from God. Some people who come into our lives are like Judas. They make decisions like Judas' that condemn them to Hell. No matter what you do to stop them from making foolish decisions, they are set in their minds and hearts to do what they want.

There is one major thing we must understand. No matter what sin we commit, we are committing that sin against God. There are consequences to sin. Just because you come to your senses and ask God for forgiveness, that does not mean that you will escape the consequences of your actions. Let me give you some examples. There are friendships lost and destroyed because of a person's actions. There are marriages destroyed because of broken vows. Parent and children relationships are ended because of wrongful actions. Character is destroyed. Reputations are tarnished. Integrity is difficult to get back if you can even get it back. Do you see my point? Pride always comes before destruction. The Bible clearly tells us this: haughtiness always comes before the fall. If I could be guaranteed to be heard, I would shout it from the mountaintop through the largest megaphone. Run away from the lusts of the flesh. Surround yourself with men and women of integrity and of great character. Stay humble. Don't disregard godly counsel. Always remember that Judas did not have a second chance. His life should put us on guard. Let it never be said that we were a Judas in someone's life or that we were a Judas to ourselves.

Judas' unrighteous life cost him eternal separation from God.

Study Guide

As we can see in the story of Judas, *"Be not deceived; God is not mocked: for whatsoever a man soweth, that shall he also reap,"* (Galatians 6:7 KJV). The story of Judas shows us that it is truly all about the condition of the heart. He walked with Jesus, traveled with Jesus, spoke with Jesus, and yet deception filled Judas' heart. Judas had the best instructor, mentor, and friend.

However, Judas chose to do the unimaginable. He betrayed the King of kings and the Lord of lords and the Redeemer of all mankind. Rather than having a life of righteousness filled with blessings, he chose destruction and death.

1. Jesus went to the mountaintop to get alone with God, setting forth an example for us to follow. Why did Jesus go to the mountaintop to get alone with the Father? And why is it important, in the life of a believer, to have time on the mountaintop daily to commune with God?

2. Read the verse Matthew 26:24 (KJV): *"The Son of man goeth as it is written of him: but woe unto that man by whom the Son of man is betrayed! it had been good for that man if he had not been born."* Why was Judas' life regrettable?

3. What was Judas doing when he took the bread that Christ offered him and ate of it at the Last Supper? And why was it so easy for Satan to enter Judas?

4. Judas had already covenanted to betray Jesus. Why was thirty shekels of silver considered an insulting price, and what was the significance of Judas throwing the pieces of silver in the faces of the priests?

5. What was the problem with Judas' heart and mind, and what did it cost Judas?

CHAPTER 9
AFTERWORD

Writing this book has been an eye-opener for me. As I have already explained, this was not a book I sat down to write. It was not premeditated. I was prepared to write on the subject of waiting on God. Every day, as we began in prayer, the Holy Spirit took over, and this book came forth. It is very clear, in the Scriptures, that God honors righteousness. Righteousness is everything to God because when you receive Jesus Christ into your heart as your Lord and Savior, you become dead to the life of unrighteousness and sin. Your mind and your eyes have been opened to the truth. The Holy Spirit is the One Who reveals all truth. The Holy Spirit is the One Who was given to us upon Jesus' return to Heaven. The Holy Spirit's hands are holding back all evil in our world. Imagine if the Holy Spirit's restraining hands were lifted. We would see the most horrific and vile sins come forth, more than what we see today. The Old and New Testaments both say, *"Be ye therefore perfect, even as your Father which is in heaven is perfect,"* (Matthew 5:48) and *"ye shall therefore be holy, for I am holy"* (Leviticus 11:45

KJV). So we can't say that we only find this in the Old Testament. Jesus repeats it in the New Testament.

The examples presented in this book of righteous living are clear, precise, and well-defined. God makes Himself perfectly clear that He honors lives of righteousness. Let me go deeper and explain why. Righteous people are obedient. God says that obedience is better than sacrifice. We can find this in the behavior of many people in the Bible. Remember Saul? He disobeyed God, and he wanted to perform the sacrifice. He wasn't a priest. He didn't have that right. He should have known better, but he chose to disobey anyway. Also, Saul had disobeyed God's direct order when he was told to kill all the Amalekites and destroy everything that belonged to them. For you and me, Obedience means following everything that God has given us to do exactly as He has instructed.

Another example is found in the story of Lot. Lot was told to leave his home with his wife and children and not turn back and look at the place they left. Lot's wife turned to look back, disobeying a direct command from God, and she was turned into a pillar of salt. I could give more examples, but you get my point.

Righteous people are not deceptive. They do not plan deceptively to get their way. They do not lie, cheat, or pretend to be righteous. In other words, they walk the walk. For instance, Ananias and Sapphira. Like the other disciples, they sold their property, and it was their choice as to what to do with the money they received. Rather than admitting the full amount of money they had received, they conspired to lie to Peter about the amount by pretending to be righteous. They were struck dead, not because they lied to Peter, but because they conspired to deceive the Holy Spirit, Who is holy and truthful. Ananias was the first to stand before Peter. By the Holy Spirit, Peter called out Ananias, asking how Satan could fill his heart and how he could lie. Ananias wasn't even given a chance to respond; he fell dead right then and there. Then his wife Sapphira came in and had no idea what had happened. Peter asked her, giving her a chance to tell the truth, if this money before them was the entire amount from the land they sold. Rather than telling the truth, she lied. Peter told her that the same men who carried out the dead body of her husband would now carry her out; she fell dead, and the men who carried out her husband carried her out. God does not take deception lightly.

Righteous people do not break the laws and the precepts of God. In the illicit affair of King David and Bathsheba, look at how they broke the commandments. Bathsheba was a married woman, and she broke the commandment *"Thou shalt not commit adultery."* She and David were equally guilty. As king, he could have taken any woman and made her his concubine or wife. It would have been okay for him to do so, but let me be clear, God never said to take more than one wife or have a concubine on the side. That was a manmade rule. God never approved of this practice. David coveted another man's wife, so he broke the commandment *"Thou shalt not covet,"* as well as *"Thou shalt not commit adultery."* He tried to lie about who fathered her baby, breaking the commandment *"Thou shalt not lie."* Then, he puts Uriah in the heat of the battle, making sure Uriah would be killed and that the child would still be passed off as Uriah's, breaking the commandment *"Thou shalt not kill."*

In taking Bathsheba, he stole another man's wife. He showed neither regard nor respect for a man risking his life for him and the kingdom, breaking the commandment *"Thou shalt not steal."* In a state of lust, King David, was looking to satisfy himself, breaking the commandment *"Thou shalt have no other gods before me."* In the moments of committing adultery, David had become his own god. You see, God says, *"Choose you this day whom you will serve."* Further, in the New Testament, Jesus said, *"No man can serve two masters: for either he will hate the one, and love the other."* The first commandment is, *"Thou shalt have no other gods before me."* This means that every time we choose, we are choosing what god we are going to serve. Are we going to serve the Living God? Are we going to serve Satan? Or are we going to serve ourselves? This is why when they chose to have sex, they chose themselves as gods, clearly breaking the first and foremost commandment. Surely, I don't need to explain that every time we do something that brings shame and embarrassment to us, it affects everyone around us, especially our family. We are not bringing honor to our mother and father when we make choices to embarrass ourselves by doing wicked and shameful things, breaking this commandment: *"Honour thy father and thy mother: that thy days may be long upon the land which the Lord thy God giveth thee."* Next, King David cooked up a scheme. He thought he could bring Uriah home and get him to sleep with Bathsheba, passing off the child he fathered with Bathsheba as Uriah's, breaking the commandment, *"Thou shalt not bear false witness against thy neighbor."* King David knew, as well as Uriah and the rest of the army, that it would have been disrespectful towards God to have relations with your wife while they were out with the Ark of the Covenant in battle. When that plan didn't work, King David got Uriah drunk on purpose, lying to him to get him to go home to his wife. Uriah acted righteously, even under the influence of alcohol. God was not going to allow King David to lie and get away with it. King David broke eight of the ten commandments for one night of sinful and lust-filled pleasure, and it cost them both. The baby they conceived died.

We have seen how God honored the widow, Abigail, Caleb, and Noah. What did these people all have in common? They were righteous before God. They obeyed everything that they were told to do. They put God first, and they honored Him with their very lives. God took notice, blessed them, honored them, preserved them and their children, and did miracles too marvelous for words.

Righteousness brings us into a friendship with God. Jesus said, *"Ye are my friends, if ye do whatsoever I command you"* (John 15:14 KJV). Jesus' words need no explanation. The ten commandments were given to us to follow and to live a righteous life. Honestly, I don't think that they are very difficult to do. We will get tempted to do what is evil, but if we are truly a friend of God, we will run away from evil just as Joseph did when he ran away from Potiphar's wife. He refused to sin against God and his master. He honored God, and he honored his master. The first half of the commandments have to do with our relationship with God, and the second half has to do with our relationship with man. Because Abraham was a righteous man, God honored him by saying, "Is there anything I shall hide from my friend Abraham?" Wow! This is what I want from God, too. This is my deepest desire, and let me tell you that God has shared things with me about events to come, protecting me from the disastrous plot prepared by the enemy. This is God's grace, mercy, and love towards His friends, the righteous. We see the same in the life of Noah. Because of his righteous living, he and his entire household were spared. In other words, he didn't participate in any of the evil going on around him. In the life of Ruth, we see that she had a choice after her husband, Naomi's son had died. She could either leave Naomi and return to her homeland now that her husband was dead or stay with Naomi. Ruth chose to stay with Naomi without hesitation. She had declared, "Your God will be my God, and your people will be my people." Ruth chose the God whom Naomi served. She cared for and took care of Naomi.

As a result, God blessed Ruth tremendously. Eventually, she met Boaz, and they got married. She became the mother of Obed, who was King David's grandfather, and she is found in the lineage of Jesus Christ, our Lord, and Savior. Because of her righteousness, she was blessed beyond measure, becoming the wife of Boaz and being the great grandmother of King David, one of the greatest kings. Another example of righteousness is Queen Esther. Queen Esther showcased her righteousness before God by doing two things. First, she determined that she would follow God, even if it meant her very life would be taken. A man or woman of righteousness stands for truth, honor, and justice. This is what distinguishes a person of great character and righteousness. They will follow God, His laws, His precepts, and His ways, regardless of what comes their way. Second, she immediately went into prayer and fasting. I find it interesting that she fasted and prayed for only three days. Let me explain. I believe Queen Esther knew in her spirit that the Lord her God would quickly deliver her enemies into her hands. God did just that. Queen Esther was elevated to a place of honor by God when she took a stand for her people. Because she chose to do the right thing and dared to approach King Artaxerxes, she saved an entire nation from being killed.

Unrighteous living is not only an offense before the face of God, but it also destroys the lives of the unrighteous. It is literally a matter of spiritual life and death. 1 Corinthians 6:9-10 (KJV) says, *"Know ye not that the unrighteous shall not inherit the kingdom of God? Be not deceived: neither fornicators, nor idolaters, nor adulterers, nor effeminate, nor abusers of themselves with mankind, Nor thieves, nor covetous, nor drunkards, nor revilers, nor extortioners, shall inherit the kingdom of God."* The Greek word for unrighteousness is "adikos" meaning "unjust; by extension wicked; by implication, treacherous; heathen:—unjust, unright-eous." I don't know about you, but I never want to be found unrighteous in the eyes of the Lord. It is a fearful thing to fall into the hands of the living God. Our God is a Consuming Fire, and our God does not play games. Do you remember Noah? The people of his day were wicked. They were diabolical, and they were lovers of themselves. God had enough, and He wiped out everything on the face of the earth. Jesus made it very clear when He said, *"But as the days of Noah were, so shall also the coming of the Son of man be. For as in the days that were before the flood they were eating and drinking, marrying and giving in marriage, until the day that Noe entered into the ark, And knew not until the flood came, and took them all away; so shall also the coming of the Son of man be"* (Matthew 24:37-39 KJV).

We live in the days of grace, which means that we can rejoice because there is still hope and forgiveness when we come to Jesus with a repentant heart. As we discussed in this book, the problem with those who were unrighteous was that they had issues of the heart. Their hearts were set on doing things the ungodly way, breaking God's laws and commands, and not caring about the things of God. They were calloused and hardened.

What kind of heart do you have? Do you have a moldable heart before God, doing His will and surrendering to His ways, or do you have a heart that cares only to do what you desire? Deuteronomy 28 speaks of the blessings that are upon the righteous. Still, it also speaks of the curses which come upon the unrighteous. The blessings and curses are not just found in Deuteronomy 28, but they are also found throughout the Bible from Genesis to Revelation. The heart you have determines whether or not you receive the blessings of God on your life and where you spend eternity. Living on this earth without the blessings of God is sad and without significance. Your life has no meaning except for a few fleeting pleasures. A life of right- eousness is lived with exuberance, excitement, passion, miracle after miracle, and longevity of life, meaning a life fully lived in honor to God, leaving behind a legacy of righteousness.

In conclusion, let us take note that we are surrounded by a great cloud of witnesses who have lived godly lives and left us an example for us to follow. The choice is ours. We have seen the lives of those who are righteous and the lives of those who are unrighteous. We see the blessings that came upon the right- eous and the curses that came upon the unrighteous. Now the choice is ours. We can live righteously and reap the benefits of living a righteous life and end it by spending eternity with God. We can hear Him say, "Well done, my good and faithful servant. You may enter in," or we can hear Him say, "Depart from me I never knew you."

I pray God opens your eyes and ears to the truth of all the blessings He has prepared for you. I pray you will bow your head right where you're at and ask the Lord Jesus Christ into your heart, allowing Him to shape and circumcise your heart, repenting of your sins, and moving forward, living a life of righteousness.

Study Guide

As we have seen throughout this book, there are lessons that we can take from each person's life that we have studied. *"Blessed are they that keep judgment, and he that doeth righteousness at all times"* (Psalm 106:3 KJV). Those who love justice and righteousness will reap the good and perfect things God has for them. Deuteronomy 28:13-14 KJV says, *"And the Lord shall make thee the head, and not the tail; and thou shalt be above only, and thou shalt not be beneath; if that thou hearken unto the commandments of the Lord thy God, which I command thee this day, to observe and to do them: And thou shalt not go aside from any of the words which I command thee this day, to the right hand, or to the left, to go after other gods to serve them."* All of us want blessings. All of us need to ask ourselves, "Am I willing to live by God's standards and His laws?" The blessings you receive depend on whether or not you choose to live a life surrendered to God. It all comes down to the condition of your heart. The choice you make to live righteously is a matter of spiritual life and death.

1. From the story of the widow and Elisha, what does the anointing of God do upon the life of one who lives righteously? What did you learn about righteous living from the widow's story?

2. In the story of Tamar, we can see that sin didn't just affect individual people, but sin also affected everyone around them. What did Tamar experience because of the men in her life who lived wickedly? What did you learn about unrighteous living from Tamar's story?

3. In the story of Abigail, we see the importance of evil speech and godly speech. Why was Abigail's approach in addressing King David significant and vital? From Abigail's story, what did you learn about godly responses and godly actions?

4. In the story of Bathsheba, we see how the choices we make affect the next generation. What made Bathsheba an accomplice in the sinful act of adultery with King David? What were the consequences due to her sin? What did you learn about the importance of choices and consequences from Bathsheba's story?

5. In the story of Caleb, we can see that the just shall live by faith. Keeping in mind that Joshua believed as Caleb did, what happened when the ten spies gave their investigative report? When did Caleb receive his inheritance? What did you learn about the role faith has in someone who lives righteously?

6. In the story of Esau, we can see that giving up a godly legacy and inheritance is foolish, and to hate it is even worse. What was the condition of Esau's heart? Explain. What was the problem in Esau giving up his birthright? What did you learn about continuing godly legacies and treasuring godly inheritances?

7. In the story of Noah, we see that Noah played a major role in saving his family. What was Noah's position in his family? What was Noah's first righteous act when he and his family got off the ark? What did that show about Noah's relationship with God? What did you learn about righteous living from the story of Noah?

8. In the story of Judas, we see that Judas was under the leadership of one of the best mentors and instructors that ever walked this earth. If Judas was truly repentant, what would have Judas done? Why was Judas' taking and eating the bread Christ offered him considered to be done in an unworthy manner? What did you learn about the heart from the story of Judas?

9. Throughout this book, we have seen that God does not take unrighteous living lightly. What determines if you will live a life of blessings and where you will spend eternity, and why? What does living a life of obedience mean? What distinguishes a person of great character and righteousness?

BY DR. TERESA ALLISSA CITRO

Raising Righteous Children

Righteous Living

Breathless Love

ABOUT THE AUTHORS

Rev. Dr. Teresa Allissa Citro, PhD, is the Chief Executive Officer of Learning Disabilities Worldwide, Inc. She is the President and Founder of Manda University. Dr. Citro is also the President and Founder of both Citro Cosmetics and Skincare and Citro Collection Fine Jewelry. Dr. Citro holds several degrees: a PhD in Education Leadership, a Doctorate in Religious Education, and a PhD in Corporate Leadership. Dr. Citro is the Founder of Blessed Hope Int'l Church and is a minister on staff. She is a well-respected authority in the field of Education/Special Education. She has written extensively in the fields of education, counseling, parenting, marriage, and Christian theology. She is the Co-Editor of two respected peer-reviewed journals on Special Education. She is the Editor-In-Chief of Everyday Life Magazine. She is the creator and co-host of the program Light of the World. Dr. Citro has received many awards for her contributions in the field of Special Education and was awarded the prestigious Presidential Lifetime Achievement Award in 2021 from the President of the United States of America. Dr. Citro is also a worldwide public speaker.

Linda A. Knowles, PhD, is the Executive Director of Thread of Hope, Inc. Dr. Knowles is also the Vice President of Academic Affairs and Dean of Theology at Manda University. She is a Professor of Theology. Dr. Knowles is also an Associate Pastor at Blessed Hope Int'l Church. She authored books, wrote periodicals, and blogs extensively on Christian theology, counseling, and godly living. She has traveled on several mission trips throughout the world. She holds a PhD in Theology and a PhD in Divinity.

Justin Noah Citro, PhD, M.Div. is the Second Vice President of the Governing Board at Thread of Hope, Inc. Dr. Citro is also the Vice President of Student Affairs at Manda University, and Associate Professor in the Theology and Divinity Departments at Manda University. He is an Associate Pastor at Blessed Hope Int'l Church. He holds his PhD in Theology and Master's Degree in Divinity.

www.ingramcontent.com/pod-product-compliance
Lightning Source LLC
Chambersburg PA
CBHW022010080426
42733CB00007B/548